P9-CQZ-988

If you're wondering why you should but this new edition of *The Political Science Student Writer's Manual*, here are eight good reasons!

1. Each common political science paper discussed in Part IV is broken down into **easy-to-follow steps** to build a strong foundation in research, thought, and writing.

2. Printed inside covers make it easier than ever to **quickly find help on an assignment or citation examples and instructions**.

3. A new Part II builds **critical thinking and writing skills** by writing *about* politics and government before writing *for* political science courses.

4. A new Chapter 9 on research is updated to reflect the **online and database research** that students do today.

5. Sections 3.2–3.4 explain and develop the intellectual tools to **make valid arguments and avoid fallacies.**

6. A new section 11.3 provides directions for preparing a brief yet competent **analysis of domestic government policy.**

7. A new section 11.4 includes a discussion of concepts and procedures for students to consider when preparing an **analysis of foreign policy.**

8. A revised Chapter 12 provides specific guidelines for **analysis of a bill currently before Congress.**

PEARSON

The Political Science Student Writer's Manual

Seventh Edition

Gregory M. Scott
University of Central Oklahoma Emeritus

Stephen M. Garrison
University of Central Oklahoma

Longman
Boston   Columbus   Indianapolis   New York   San Francisco   Upper Saddle River
Amsterdam   Cape Town   Dubai   London   Madrid   Milan   Munich   Paris   Montreal   Toronto
Delhi   Mexico City   São Paulo   Sydney   Hong Kong   Seoul   Singapore   Taipei   Tokyo

Acquisitions Editor: Reid Hester
Project Editor: Tony Magyar
Senior Marketing Manager: Lindsey Prudhomme
Production Manager: Fran Russello
Project Coordination, Text Design, and Electronic Page Makeup: Karpagam Jagadeesan/
    PreMediaGlobal
Cover Design Manager: Jayne Conte
Cover Designer: Bruce Kenselaar
Printer and Binder: Edwards Brothers
Cover Printer: Lehigh Phoenix

Copyright © 2012, 2008, 2006 by Pearson Education, Inc.

Library of Congress Cataloging-in-Publication Data

Scott, Gregory M.
   The poltical science student writer's manual / Gregory M. Scott,
Stephen M. Garrison.—7th ed.
       p.   cm.
   Includes bibliographical references and index.
   ISBN-13: 978-0-205-83012-1 (alk. paper)
   ISBN-10: 0-205-83012-9 (alk. paper)
   1. Political science—Authorship—Style manuals.   2. Political science—Research—Handbooks, manuals, etc.   3. Academic writing—Handbooks, manuals, etc.   4. Report writing—Handbooks, manuals, etc.   I. Garrison, Stephen M.   II. Title.
   JA86.S39 2012
   808'.06632—dc22

                                                                    2010050258

1 2 3 4 5 6 7 8 9 10—EB—14 13 12 11

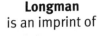

Longman
is an imprint of

www.pearsonhighered.com

ISBN-10: 0-205-83012-9
ISBN-13: 978-0-205-83012-1

Brief Contents

To the Teacher

This book helps you deal with three problems commonly faced by teachers of political science:

- Students increasingly need specific directions to produce a good paper.
- Political scientists, as always, want to teach political science, not English.
- Students do not yet understand fully how—and why—to avoid plagiarism.

How many times have you assigned papers in your political science classes and found yourself teaching the basics of writing—not only in terms of content but form and grammar as well? This text, which may either accompany the primary text you assign in any class or stand on its own, allows you to assign one of the types of papers described in Parts 2, 3, and 4, with the knowledge that virtually everything the student needs to know, from grammar to sources of information to reference style, is in this one volume.

Part 1 helps you to spend more time teaching political science and less time teaching English. It includes (1) a concise guide to writing well, (2) a summary of the most troublesome English grammar rules, (3) proper political science college paper formats, and (4) extensive instruction and examples on how to cite sources according to specifications published by the American Political Science Association (APSA).

Also, this book may well be your best insurance against plagiarism, for two reasons. First, Section 5.5 provides a detailed, practical explanation of what plagiarism is and how to avoid it. Second, the writing assignments in Parts 2, 3, and 4 of this manual provide very specific directions that make it much more difficult for students simply to appropriate uncredited material, even from the Internet, where, as you know, it is becoming easier for students to download relevant material and then modify it (insufficiently) for their own purposes.

New to This Edition

In addition, although the previous edition is quite different from its predecessor, this seventh edition is the *most substantial revision* of *The Political Science Student Writer's Manual* yet undertaken. Among the scores of changes throughout the volume, you will find the following *entirely new material*:

- Sections 3.2–3.4 political science students with the intellectual tools philosophers use to make valid and cogent arguments and avoid fallacies.
- Section 6.4 teaches students how to contribute effectively to a *political blog*.
- Section 7.1 prepares students to astutely analyze political *campaign commercials*.
- Section 11.3 provides students in introductory class with directions for preparing a brief yet competent *analysis of a domestic government policy*.
- Section 11.4 includes a discussion of concepts and procedures for students to consider when preparing an *analysis of a specific foreign policy*.
- Chapter 12 provides students in advance courses focusing on Congress and on the legislative process with specific guidelines for *analyzing a bill currently before Congress*.

Acknowledgments

We'd like to thank the following reviewers for their helpful comments and suggestions: Napp Nazworth, The University of Georgia; Sara Parker, Cal State University—East Bay; and Zachary Shirkey, St. John Fisher College.

We hope you find that the seventh edition helps you in your efforts to teach political science. We wish you the best in your endeavors, and we welcome your comments.

GREG SCOTT
STEVE GARRISON

To the Student

We have designed this book to help you do two things: (1) improve your writing and (2) learn political science. Part 1 addresses fundamental concerns of all writers, exploring the reasons why we write, describing the writing process itself, and examining those elements of grammar, style, and punctuation that cause the most confusion among writers in general. A vital concern throughout this part, and the rest of the book as well, is the three-way interrelationship among writer, topic, and audience. Our discussion of this relationship aims at building your self-confidence as you clarify your writing objectives.

Writing is not a magical process beyond the control of most people. It is instead a series of interconnected skills that any writer can improve with practice, and the end result of this practice is power. This manual treats the act of writing not as an empty exercise undertaken only to produce a grade but as a powerful learning tool and the primary medium by which political scientists accomplish their goals. Chapter 3 explains the importance of formatting your writing properly; supplies you with format models for title pages, tables of contents, and so on; and then demonstrates how to cite sources and how to use source material ethically.

Parts 2, 3, and 4 of the book offer you general help in formulating and researching political science writing projects. We have based these assignments on the types of work political scientists actually do, both as academic professionals and as contributing citizens in local and in national political communities. The assignments will test your ability to think critically and come up with and express ideas that will improve all our lives.

GREG SCOTT
STEVE GARRISON

Introduction: Welcome to the Study of Politics and Government

The purpose of this book is to help you express your thoughts about things in general and about politics and government in particular. Because your success in writing will depend as much on the knowledge of your subject as upon the way you express yourself, it may be helpful to begin by taking a few brief moments to reflect on your subjects—politics and government—so that you can discover what you are taking college courses to learn: what they are *really* all about.

What has your own experience told you about the political aspects of life? You have already experienced, for example, countless ways that politics and government affect your daily life. Your freedom to select the school you want to attend, your confidence in the quality of canned tuna that you buy, the amount that is taken from your paycheck every week, all these aspects of your life and many more are determined by presidents, members of Congress, justices, and hundreds of other government officials. But politics is more than just laws and regulations. It is a fundamental aspect of human existence so pervasive in our lives that we find it difficult to define.

Political scientists like to try to define politics, and they have done this in many ways. According to some of the most famous definitions, politics is

- The science of who gets what, when, and how (Harold Lasswell, *Politics: Who Gets What, When, How*, 1936)
- The authoritative allocation of values (David Easton, *The Political System*, 1953)
- The activity by which differing interests within a given unit of rule are conciliated by giving them a share in power in proportion to their importance to . . . the whole community (Bernard Crick, *In Defense of Politics*, 1962)
- The processes by which human efforts toward attaining social goals are steered and coordinated (Karl Deutsch, *The Nerves of Government: Models of Political Communication and Control*, 1963)
- The process of making government policies (Austin Ranney, *Governing: An Introduction to Political Science*, 1990)
- The art of looking for trouble, finding it everywhere, diagnosing it incorrectly, and applying the wrong remedies (Groucho Marx)

In spite of the differences among these definitions, several qualities are common to them all:

- Politics is *relational*, that is, it has to do with relationships among people or groups of people.

1

- Politics concerns *interests and power*. The signature of political activity is the attempt on someone's part to further his or her own interest, increase his or her own power, or to reduce the influence of someone else.
- Politics is *dynamic*. This means that politics is not a snapshot of an event or a place in time, nor is it a collection of snapshots. It is a process or an activity that is perpetually in motion, constantly changing, continually expressing, transforming, and conforming to the people, trends, and events through which it operates.

Politics is often a chaotic clash of interests and values all striving for acceptance or dominance. People in politics strive to construct an order that will allow them to obtain the goals they seek, an order that works at all levels, including the micro- (small groups such as family members), the medial- (larger groups like community associations), and the macrolevel (states, provinces, and nations). This means that politics is a way in which we meet our emotional needs for unity and individuality, as well as our physical needs. Perhaps it is fair, then, to say that *politics is the word we use to describe the way human beings normally relate to each other*. And if this is the case, then defining government is relatively easy. *Government is the means we use to bring order to politics*.

Government is a forum and an authoritative structure for making, interpreting, and enforcing the rules through which politics operates in society. Government is the laws, institutions, and processes that set the rules and create the mechanisms through which human relations are publicly carried out. Governments make laws about the limits of marriage, proper conduct in family life, business relations, use of the physical environment, national defense, and other matters. In its most basic sense, it is the set of rules and institutions that establish the order within which politics is conducted in society.

Before we end this introduction, let's take one more step. Because this book is *The Political Science Student Writer's Manual*, let's define political science. *Political science is the creative analytical study of politics and government*. To be analytical is to try, as objectively as possible, to understand how something works. To analyze something is to look at it as a whole—from various viewpoints—and to examine its parts to see how they affect each other. When we draw conclusions from what we observe we necessarily make interpretations, and making interpretations always requires creativity. Creativity is the heart of political science, as it is of all science.

Creativity will probably always seem a bit mysterious. Speaking of the great French Impressionist painter Paul Cezanne, psychologist Rollo May commented:

> Cezanne sees a tree. He sees it in a way no one else has ever seen it. He experiences, as he no doubt would have said, "being grasped by the tree." The arching grandeur of the tree, the mothering spread, the delicate balance as the tree grips the earth—all these and many more characteristics of the tree are absorbed into his perception and are felt throughout his nervous structure. These are part of the vision he experiences. This vision involves an omission of some aspects of the scene and a greater emphasis on other aspects and the ensuing rearrangement of the whole; but it is more than the sum of all these. Primarily it is a vision that is now not the tree, but Tree; the concrete tree Cezanne looked at is formed

into the essence of tree. However original and unrepeatable his vision is, it is still a vision of all trees triggered by his encounter with this particular one.

The painting that issues out of this encounter between a human being, Cezanne, and an objective reality, the tree, is literally new, unique, and original. Something is born, comes into being, something that did not exist before—which is as good a definition of creativity as we can get. Thereafter, everyone who looks at the painting with intensity of awareness and lets it speak to him or her will see the tree with the unique powerful movement, the intimacy between the tree and the landscape, and the architectural beauty which literally did not exist in our relation with trees until Cezanne experienced and painted them. I can say without exaggeration that I never really *saw* a tree until I had seen and absorbed Cezanne's paintings of them. (May 1975, 77–78)

When it is successful, political science does for our understanding of politics what Cezanne's representation of a tree does for our perception of trees. So now, begin your quest. Write about politics and government. Write well, and in so doing enjoy the marvelous adventure that the creative exploration of politics and government has in store for you.

Part I
Before you Write: Review the Basics

CHAPTER 1
Seize the Day: Write!

1.1 Focus on Your Goal: Writing to Learn

Writing is a way of ordering your experience. Think about it. No matter what you are writing—it may be a paper for your American government class, a short story, a limerick, a grocery list—you are putting pieces of your world together in new ways and making yourself freshly conscious of those pieces. This is one of the reasons why writing is so hard. From the infinite welter of data that your mind continually processes and locks in your memory, you are selecting only certain items significant to the task at hand, relating them to other items, and phrasing them with a new coherence. You are mapping a part of your universe that has hitherto been unknown territory. You are gaining a little more control over the processes by which you interact with the world around you.

This is why the act of writing, no matter what its result, is never insignificant. It is always *communication*—if not with another human being, then with yourself. It is a way of making a fresh connection with your world.

Writing therefore is also one of the best ways to learn. This statement may sound odd at first. If you are an unpracticed writer, you may share a common notion that the only purpose of writing is to express what you already know or think. According to this view, any learning that you as a writer might have experienced has already occurred by the time your pen meets the paper; your task is thus to inform and even surprise the reader. But, if you are a practiced writer, you know that at any moment as you write, you are capable of surprising yourself. And it is that surprise that you look for: the shock of seeing what happens in your own mind when you drop an old, established opinion into a batch of new facts or bump into a cherished belief from a different angle. Writing synthesizes new understanding for the writer. E. M. Forster's famous question "How do I know what I think until I see what I say?" is one that all of us could ask. We make meaning as we write, jolting ourselves by little, surprising discoveries into a larger and more interesting universe.

The Irony of Writing. Good writing, especially good writing about politics, helps the reader become aware of the ironies and paradoxes of human existence. One such paradox is that good writing expresses both that which is unique about the writer and that which the writer shares with every human being. Many of our most famous political statements share this double attribute of mirroring the singular and the ordinary simultaneously. For example, read the following excerpt from President

Franklin Roosevelt's first inaugural address, spoken on March 4, 1933, in the middle of the Great Depression, and then answer this question: Is Roosevelt's speech famous because its expression is extraordinary or because it appeals to something that is basic to every human being?

> This is pre-eminently the time to speak the truth, the whole truth, frankly and boldly. Nor need we shrink from honestly facing conditions in our country today. This great nation will endure as it has endured, will revive and will prosper.
>
> So first of all let me assert my firm belief that the only thing we have to fear is fear itself—nameless, unreasoning, unjustified terror which paralyzes needed efforts to convert retreat into advance.
>
> In every dark hour of our national life a leadership of frankness and vigor has met with that understanding and support of the people themselves which is essential to victory. I am convinced that you will again give that support to leadership in these critical days.
>
> In such a spirit on my part and on yours we face our common difficulties. They concern, thank God, only material things. Values have shrunken to fantastic levels; taxes have risen; our ability to pay has fallen; government of all kinds is faced by serious curtailment of income; the means of exchange are frozen in the currents of trade; the withered leaves of industrial enterprise lie on every side; farmers find no markets for their produce; the savings of many years in thousands of families are gone.
>
> More important, a host of unemployed citizens face the grim problem of existence, and an equally great number toil with little return. Only a foolish optimist can deny the dark realities of the moment.
>
> Yet our distress comes from no failure of substance. We are stricken by no plague of locusts. Compared with the perils which our forefathers conquered because they believed and were not afraid, we have still much to be thankful for. Nature still offers her bounty and human efforts have multiplied it. Plenty is at our doorstep, but a generous use of it languishes in the very sight of the supply. . . .
>
> The measure of the restoration lies in the extent to which we apply social values more noble than mere monetary profit.
>
> Happiness lies not in the mere possession of money; it lies in the joy of achievement, in the thrill of creative effort.
>
> The joy and moral stimulation of work no longer must be forgotten in the mad chase of evanescent profits. These dark days will be worth all they cost us if they teach us that our true destiny is not to be ministered unto but to minister to ourselves and to our fellow-men. (Roosevelt 1963, 240)

The help that writing gives us with learning and with controlling what we learn is one of the major reasons why your political science instructors will require a great deal of writing from you. Learning the complex and diverse world of the political scientist takes more than a passive ingestion of facts. You have to understand the processes of government, and come to grips with social issues and with your own attitudes toward them. When you write in a class on American government or public policy, you are entering into the world of political scientists in the same way they do—by testing theory against fact and fact against belief.

Writing is the means of entering political life. Virtually everything that happens in politics happens first on paper. Documents are wrestled into shape before their contents can affect the public. Great speeches are written before they are spoken. The written word has helped bring slaves to freedom, end wars, and shape the values of nations. Often, in politics as elsewhere, gaining recognition for ourselves and our ideas depends less on what we say than on how we say it. Accurate and persuasive writing is absolutely vital to the political scientist.

EXERCISE 1.1   Learn by Writing

One way of testing the notion that writing is a powerful learning tool is by rewriting your notes from a recent class lecture. The type of class does not matter; it can be history, chemistry, advertising, whatever. If possible, choose a difficult class, one in which you are feeling somewhat unsure of the material and for which you have taken copious notes.

As you rewrite, provide the transitional elements (connecting phrases such as *in order to,* *because of, and, but,* and *however*) that you were unable to supply in class because of the press of time. Furnish your own examples or illustrations of the ideas expressed in the lecture.

This experiment will force you to supply necessary coherence to your own thought processes. See if your increased understanding of the lecture material does not more than compensate for the time it takes you to rewrite the notes.

Challenge Yourself.   There is no way around it: writing is a struggle. Did you think you were the only one to feel this way? Take heart! Writing is hard for everybody, great writers included. Bringing order to the world is never easy. Isaac Bashevis Singer, winner of the 1978 Nobel Prize in literature, once wrote: "I believe in miracles in every area of life except writing. Experience has shown me that there are no miracles in writing. The only thing that produces good writing is hard work" (quoted in Lunsford and Connors 1992, 2).

Hard work was evident in the words of John F. Kennedy's inaugural address. Each word was crafted to embed an image in the listeners' mind. As you read the following excerpt from Kennedy's speech, what images does it evoke? Historians tend to consider a president "great" when his words live longer than his deeds in the minds of the people. Do you think this will be—or has been—true of Kennedy?

We observe today not a victory of party but a celebration of freedom—symbolizing an end as well as a beginning—signifying renewal as well as change. For I have sworn before you and Almighty God the same solemn oath our forebears prescribed nearly a century and three-quarters ago.

The world is very different now. For man holds in his mortal hands the power to abolish all forms of human poverty and all forms of human life. And yet the same revolutionary beliefs for which our forebears fought are still at issue around the globe—the belief that the rights of man come not from the generosity of the state but from the hand of God.

We dare not forget today that we are the heirs of that first revolution. Let the word go forth from this time and place, to friend and foe alike, that the torch has been passed to a new generation of Americans—born in this century, tempered by war, disciplined by a hard and bitter peace, proud of our ancient heritage—and unwilling to witness or permit the slow undoing of those human rights to which this nation has always been committed, and to which we are committed today at home and around the world. . . .

In the long history of the world, only a few generations have been granted the role of defending freedom in its hours of maximum danger. I do not shrink from this responsibility—I welcome it. I do not believe that any of us would exchange places with any other people or any other generation. The energy, the faith, the devotion which we bring to this endeavor will light our country and all who serve it—and the glow from that fire can truly light the world.

And so, my fellow Americans: ask not what your country can do for you—ask what you can do for your country.

My fellow citizens of the world: ask not what America will do for you, but what together we can do for the freedom of man. (Kennedy 1963, 688–89)

One reason that writing is difficult is that it is not actually a single activity at all but a process consisting of several activities that can overlap, with two or more sometimes operating simultaneously as you labor to organize and phrase your thoughts. (We will discuss these activities later in this chapter.) The writing process tends to be sloppy for everyone, an often-frustrating search for meaning and for the best way to articulate that meaning.

Frustrating though that search may sometimes be, it need not be futile. Remember this: the writing process uses skills that we all have. The ability to write, in other words, is not some magical competence bestowed on the rare, fortunate individual. Although few of us may achieve the proficiency of Isaac Bashevis Singer or John F. Kennedy, we are all capable of phrasing thoughts clearly and in a well-organized fashion. But learning how to do so takes practice.

The one sure way to improve your writing is to write.

One of the toughest but most important jobs in writing is to maintain enthusiasm for your writing project. Such commitment may sometimes be hard to achieve, given the difficulties that are inherent in the writing process and that can be made worse when the project is unappealing at first glance. How, for example, can you be enthusiastic about having to write a paper analyzing campaign financing for the 1998 congressional elections, when you have never once thought about campaign finances and can see no use in doing so now?

One of the worst mistakes that unpracticed student writers make is to fail to assume responsibility for keeping themselves interested in their writing. No matter how hard it may seem at first to drum up interest in your topic, you have to do it— that is, if you want to write a paper you can be proud of, one that contributes useful material and a fresh point of view to the topic. One thing is guaranteed: if you are bored with your writing, your reader will be, too. So what can you do to keep your interest and energy level high?

Challenge yourself. Think of the paper not as an assignment but as a piece of writing that has a point to make. To get this point across persuasively is the real reason you are writing, not because a teacher has assigned you a project. If someone were to ask you why you are writing your paper and your immediate, unthinking response is, "Because I've been given a writing assignment" or "Because I want a good grade" or some other nonanswer along these lines, your paper may be in trouble.

If, on the other hand, your first impulse is to explain the challenge of your main point—"I'm writing to show how campaign finance reform will benefit every taxpayer in America"—then you are thinking usefully about your topic.

Maintain Self-Confidence.   Having confidence in your ability to write well about your topic is essential for good writing. This does not mean that you will always know what the result of a particular writing activity will be. In fact, you have to cultivate your ability to tolerate a high degree of uncertainty while weighing evidence, testing hypotheses, and experimenting with organizational strategies and wording. Be ready for temporary confusion and for seeming dead ends, and remember that every writer faces these obstacles. It is out of your struggle to combine fact with fact, to buttress conjecture with evidence, that order will arise.

Do not be intimidated by the amount and quality of work that others have already done in your field of inquiry. The array of opinion and evidence that confronts you in the literature can be confusing. But remember that no important topic is ever exhausted. There are always gaps—questions that have not been satisfactorily explored in either the published research or the prevailing popular opinion. It is in these gaps that you establish your own authority, your own sense of control.

Remember that the various stages of the writing process reinforce each other. Establishing a solid motivation strengthens your sense of confidence about the project, which in turn influences how successfully you organize your material and write. If you start out well, use good work habits, and allow ample time for the various activities to coalesce, you should produce a paper that will reflect your best work, one that your audience will find both readable and useful.

1.2   Get into the Flow of Writing

The Nature of the Process.   As you engage in the writing process, you are doing many things at once. While planning, you are, no doubt, defining the audience for your paper at the same time that you are thinking about its purpose. As you draft the paper, you may organize your next sentence while revising the one you have just written. Different parts of the writing process overlap, and much of the difficulty of writing occurs because so many things happen at once. Through practice—in other words, through *writing*—it is possible to learn to control those parts of the process that can in fact be controlled and to encourage those mysterious, less controllable activities.

No two people go about writing in exactly the same way. It is important to recognize the routines—modes of thought as well as individual exercises—that help you negotiate the process successfully. It is also important to give yourself as much time as possible to complete the process. Procrastination is one of the writer's greatest enemies. It saps confidence, undermines energy, and destroys concentration. Writing regularly and following a well-planned schedule as closely as possible often make the difference between a successful paper and an embarrassment.

Although the various parts of the writing process are interwoven, there is naturally a general order in the work of writing. You have to start somewhere! What follows is a description of the various stages of the writing process—planning, drafting, revising, editing, and proofreading—along with suggestions on how to approach each most successfully.

1.3   Plan

Planning includes all activities that lead to the writing of the first draft of a paper. The particular activities in this stage differ from person to person. Some writers, for instance, prefer to compile a formal outline before writing the draft. Others perform brief writing exercises to jump-start their imaginations. Some draw diagrams; some doodle. Later, we will look at a few starting strategies, and you can determine which may help you.

Now, however, let us discuss certain early choices that all writers must make during the planning stage. These choices concern *topic, purpose, and audience*, elements that make up the writing context, or the terms under which we all write. Every time you write, even if you are only writing a diary entry or a note to the milkman, these elements are present. You may not give conscious consideration to all of them in each piece of writing that you do, but it is extremely important to think carefully about them when writing a political science paper. Some or all of these defining elements may be dictated by your assignment, yet you will always have a degree of control over them.

1.4   Select a Topic

No matter how restrictive an assignment may seem, there is no reason to feel trapped by it. Within any assigned subject you can find a range of topics to explore. What you are looking for is a topic that engages your own interest. Let your curiosity be your guide. If, for example, you have been assigned the subject of campaign finances, then guide yourself to find some issues concerning the topic that interests you. (For example, how influential are campaign finances in the average state senate race? What would be the repercussions of limiting financial contributions from special interest groups?) Any good topic comes with a set of questions; you may well find that your interest increases if you simply begin asking questions. One strong recommendation: ask your questions *on paper*. Like most mental activities, the process of exploring your way through a topic is transformed when you write down your thoughts as they come, instead of letting them fly through your mind unrecorded. Remember the words of Louis Agassiz: "A pen is often the best of eyes" (1958, 106).

Although it is vital to be interested in your topic, you do not have to know much about it at the outset of your investigation. In fact, having too heartfelt a commitment to a topic can be an impediment to writing about it; emotions can get in the way of objectivity. It is often better to choose a topic that has piqued your interest yet remained something of a mystery to you—a topic discussed in one of your classes, perhaps, or mentioned on television or in a conversation with friends.

1.5   Narrow the Topic

The task of narrowing your topic offers you a tremendous opportunity to establish a measure of control over the writing project. It is up to you to hone your topic to just the right shape and size to suit both your own interests and the requirements of the assignment. Do a good job of it, and you will go a long way toward guaranteeing yourself sufficient motivation and confidence for the tasks ahead. However, if you do not do it well, somewhere along the way you may find yourself directionless and out of energy.

Generally, the first topics that come to your mind will be too large for you to handle in your research paper. For example, the subject of a national income security policy has recently generated a tremendous number of news reports. Yet despite all the attention, there is still plenty of room for you to investigate the topic on a level that has real meaning for you and that does not merely recapitulate the published research. What about an analysis of how one of the proposed income security policies might affect insurance costs in a locally owned company?

The problem with most topics is not that they are too narrow or have been too completely explored, but rather that they are so rich that it is often difficult to choose the most useful way to address them. Take some time to narrow your topic. Think through the possibilities that occur to you and, as always, jot down your thoughts.

Students in an undergraduate course on political theory were told to write an essay of 2,500 words on one of the following issues. Next to each general topic is an example of how students narrowed it into a manageable paper topic.

GENERAL TOPIC	NARROWED TOPIC
Barack Obama	Obama's strategy in the war in Afghanistan.
Freedom	A comparison of Jean Jacques Rousseau's concept of freedom with that of John Locke
Interest Groups	The political power of the National Rifle Association
Bart Simpson	Bart Simpson's political ideology

EXERCISE 1.2   Narrowing Topics

Without doing research, see how you can narrow the following general topics:

EXAMPLE

General topic	The United Nations
Narrowed topics	The United Nations' intervention in civil wars
	The United Nations' attempts to end starvation
	The role of the United Nations in stopping nuclear proliferation

GENERAL TOPICS

War in Iraq	Gun control	Freedom of marriage
International terrorism	Political corruption	Abortion right
Education	Military spending	
Freedom of speech	The budget deficit	

1.6 Find a Thesis

As you plan your writing, be on the lookout for an idea that can serve as your thesis. A *thesis* is not a fact, which can be immediately verified by data, but an assertion worth discussing, an argument with more than one possible conclusion. Your thesis sentence will reveal to your reader not only the argument you have chosen but also your orientation toward it and the conclusion that your paper will attempt to prove.

In looking for a thesis, you are doing many jobs at once:

1. You are limiting the amount and kind of material that you must cover, thus making them manageable.
2. You are increasing your own interest in the narrowing field of study.
3. You are working to establish your paper's purpose, the reason you are writing about your topic. (If the only reason you can see for writing is to earn a good grade, then you probably won't!)
4. You are establishing your notion of who your audience is and what sort of approach to the subject might best catch its interest.

In short, you are gaining control over your writing context. For this reason, it is a good idea to come up with a thesis early on, a *working thesis*, which will very probably change as your thinking deepens but which will allow you to establish a measure of order in the planning stage.

The Thesis Sentence.   The introduction of your paper will contain a sentence that expresses the task that you intend to accomplish. This *thesis sentence* communicates your main idea, the one you are going to prove, defend, or illustrate. It sets up an expectation in the reader's mind that it is your job to satisfy. But, in the planning stage, a thesis sentence is more than just the statement that informs your reader of your goal: it is a valuable tool to help you narrow your focus and confirm in your own mind your paper's purpose.

Developing a Thesis.   Students in a class on public policy analysis were assigned a twenty-page paper on a problem currently being faced by the municipal authorities in their own city. The choice of the problem was left to the students. One, Richard Cory, decided to investigate the problem posed by the large number of abandoned buildings in a downtown neighborhood through which he drove on his way to the university. His first working thesis was as follows:

Abandoned houses result in negative social effects to the city.

The problem with this thesis, as Richard found out, was that it was not an idea that could be argued, but rather a fact that could be easily corroborated by the sources he began to consult. As he read reports from such groups as the Urban Land Institute and the City Planning Commission, and talked with representatives from the Community Planning Department, he began to get interested in the dilemma his city faced in responding to the problem of abandoned buildings. Richard's second working thesis was as follows:

Removal of abandoned buildings is a major problem facing the city.

While his second thesis narrowed the topic somewhat and gave Richard an opportunity to use material from his research, there was still no real comment attached to it. It still stated a bare fact, easily proved. At this point, Richard became interested in the even narrower topic of how building removal should best be handled. He found that the major issue was funding and that different civic groups favored different methods of accomplishing this. As Richard explored the arguments for and against the various funding plans, he began to feel that one of them might be best for the city. As a result, Richard developed his third working thesis:

Assessing a demolition fee on each property offers a viable solution to the city's building removal problem.

Note how this thesis narrows the focus of Richard's paper even further than the other two had, while also presenting an arguable hypothesis. It tells Richard what he has to do in his paper, just as it tells his readers what to expect.

At some time during your preliminary thinking on a topic, you should consult a library to see how much published work on your issue exists. This search has at least two benefits:

1. It acquaints you with a body of writing that will become very important in the research phase of your paper.
2. It gives you a sense of how your topic is generally addressed by the community of scholars you are joining. Is the topic as important as you think it is? Has there been so much research on the subject as to make your inquiry, in its present formulation, irrelevant?

As you go about determining your topic, remember that one goal of your political science writing in college is always to enhance your own understanding of the political process, to build an accurate model of the way politics works. Let this goal help you to direct your research into those areas that you know are important to your knowledge of the discipline.

1.7   Define a Purpose

There are many ways to classify the purposes of writing, but in general most writing is undertaken either to inform or to persuade an audience. The goal of informative, or expository, writing is simply to impart information about a particular subject, whereas the aim of persuasive writing is to convince your reader of your point of view on an issue. The distinction between expository and persuasive writing is not hard and fast, and most writing in political science has elements of both types. Most effective writing, however, is clearly focused on either exposition or persuasion. Position papers (arguments for adopting particular policies), for example, are designed to persuade, whereas policy analysis papers (Chapter 9) are meant to inform. When you begin writing, consciously select a primary approach of exposition or persuasion, and then set out to achieve that goal.

EXERCISE 1.3   To Explain or to Persuade

Can you tell from the titles of these two papers, both on the same topic, which is an expository paper and which is a persuasive paper?

1. Social Services Funding in the Second George W. Bush Administration
2. How the Second George W. Bush Administration Shifted Shares of Wealth in America

Again taking up the subject of campaign finances, let us assume that you must write a paper explaining how finances were managed in the 2004 Republican presidential campaign. If you are writing an expository paper, your task could be to describe as coherently and impartially as possible the methods by which the Republicans administered their campaign funds. If, however, you are attempting to convince your readers that the 2004 Republican campaign finances were criminally mismanaged by an elected official, you are writing to persuade, and your strategy will be radically different. Persuasive writing seeks to influence the opinions of its audience toward its subject.

Learn what you want to say. By the time you write your final draft, you must have a very sound notion of the point you wish to argue. If, as you write that final draft, someone were to ask you to state your thesis, you should be able to give a satisfactory answer with a minimum of delay and no prompting. If, on the other hand, you have to hedge your answer because you cannot easily express your thesis, you may not yet be ready to write a final draft. You may have to write a draft or two or engage in various prewriting activities to form a secure understanding of your task.

EXERCISE 1.4   Knowing What You Want to Say

Two writers have been asked to state the thesis of their papers. Which one better understands the writing task?

Writer 1:   "My paper is about tax reform for the middle class."

(Continued)

EXERCISE 1.4   Knowing What You Want to Say   *(Continued)*

Writer 2:   "My paper argues that tax reform for the middle class would be unfair to the upper and lower classes, who would then have to share more responsibility for the cost of government."

Watch out for bias! There is no such thing as pure objectivity. You are not a machine. No matter how hard you may try to produce an objective paper, the fact is that every choice you make as you write is influenced to some extent by your personal beliefs and opinions. What you tell your readers is truth, in other words, is influenced, sometimes without your knowledge, by a multitude of factors: your environment, upbringing, and education; your attitude toward your audience; your political affiliation; your race and gender; your career goals; and your ambitions for the paper you are writing. The influence of such factors can be very subtle, and it is something you must work to identify in your own writing as well as in the writing of others in order not to mislead or to be misled. Remember that one of the reasons for writing is *self-discovery.* The writing you will do in political science classes—as well as the writing you will do for the rest of your life—will give you a chance to discover and confront honestly your own views on your subjects. Responsible writers keep an eye on their own biases and are honest about them with their readers.

1.8   Define Your Audience

In any class that requires you to write, you may sometimes find it difficult to remember that the point of your writing is not simply to jump through the technical hoops imposed by the assignment. The point is *communication*—the transmission of your knowledge and your conclusions to readers in a way that suits you. Your task is to pass on to your readers the spark of your own enthusiasm for your topic. Readers who were indifferent to your topic before reading your paper should look at it in a new way after finishing it. This is the great challenge of writing: to enter into a reader's mind and leave behind both new knowledge and new questions.

It is tempting to think that most writing problems would be solved if the writer could view the writing as if another person had produced it. The discrepancy between the understanding of the writer and that of the audience is the single greatest impediment to accurate communication. To overcome this barrier you must consider your audience's needs. By the time you begin drafting, most, if not all, of your ideas will have begun to attain coherent shape in your mind, so that virtually any words with which you try to express those ideas will reflect your thought accurately—to you. Your readers, however, do not already hold the conclusions that you have so painstakingly achieved. If you omit from your writing the material that is necessary to complete your readers' understanding of your argument, they may well be unable to supply that information themselves.

The potential for misunderstanding is present for any audience, whether it is made up of general readers, experts in the field, or your professor, who is reading in part to see how well you have mastered the constraints that govern the relationship between writer and reader. Make your presentation as complete as possible, bearing in mind your audience's knowledge of your topic.

1.9   Think Creatively

We have discussed various methods of selecting and narrowing the topic of a paper. As your focus on a specific topic sharpens, you will naturally begin to think about the kinds of information that will go into the paper. In the case of papers that do not require formal research, this material will come largely from your own recollections. Indeed, one of the reasons instructors assign such papers is to convince you of the incredible richness of your memory, the vastness and variety of the "database" that you have accumulated and that, moment by moment, you continue to build.

So vast is your hoard of information that it can sometimes be difficult to find within it the material that would best suit your paper. In other words, finding out what you already know about a topic is not always easy. *Invention*, a term borrowed from classical rhetoric, refers to the task of discovering, or recovering from memory, such information. As we write, we go through some sort of invention procedure that helps us explore our topic. Some writers seem to have little problem coming up with material; others need more help. Over the centuries, writers have devised different exercises that can help locate useful material housed in memory. We will look at a few of these briefly.

Freewriting.   *Freewriting* is an activity that forces you to get something down on paper. There is no waiting around for inspiration. Instead, you set a time limit—perhaps three to five minutes—and write for that length of time without stopping, not even to lift the pen from the paper or your hands from the keyboard. Focus on the topic, and do not let the difficulty of finding relevant material stop you from writing. If necessary, you may begin by writing, over and over, some seemingly useless phrase, such as, "I cannot think of anything to write," or perhaps the name of your topic. Eventually, something else will occur to you. (It is surprising how long a three-minute period of freewriting can seem to last!) At the end of the freewriting, look over what you have produced for anything you might be able to use. Much of the writing will be unusable, but there might be an insight or two that you did not know you had.

In addition to its ability to help you recover usable material from your memory for your paper, freewriting has certain other benefits. First, it takes little time, which means that you may repeat the exercise as often as you like. Second, it breaks down some of the resistance that stands between you and the act of writing. There is no initial struggle to find something to say; you just write.

For his second-year American government class, Bill Alexander had to write a paper on some aspects of local government. Bill, who felt his understanding of local government was slight, began the job of finding a topic that interested him with two minutes of freewriting. Thinking about local government, Bill wrote steadily for this period without lifting his pen from the paper. Here is the result of his freewriting:

> Okay, okay local government. Local, what does that mean? Like police? Chamber of Commerce? the mayor—whoever that is? judges? I got that parking ticket last year, went to court, had to pay it anyway, bummer. Maybe trace what happens to a single parking ticket—and my money.

Find out the public officials who deal with it, from the traffic cop who gives it out to wherever it ends up. Point would be, what? Point point point. To find out how much the local government spends to give out and process a $35 parking ticket—how much do they really make after expenses, and where does that money go? Have to include cop's salary? judge's? Printing costs for ticket? Salary for clerk or whoever deals only with ticket. Is there somebody who lives whole life only processing traffic tickets? Are traffic tickets and parking tickets handled differently? Assuming the guy fights it. Maybe find out the difference in revenue between a contested and an uncontested ticket? Lots of phone calls to make. Who? Where to start?

Brainstorming.   *Brainstorming* is simply the process of making a list of ideas about a topic. It can be done quickly and at first without any need to order items in a coherent pattern. The point is to write down everything that occurs to you as quickly and briefly as possible, using individual words or short phrases. Once you have a good-sized list of items, you can then group them according to relationships that you see among them. Brainstorming thus allows you to uncover both ideas stored in your memory and useful associations among those ideas.

A professor in an international politics class asked his students to write a 700-word paper, in the form of a letter to be translated and published in a Warsaw newspaper, giving Polish readers useful advice about living in a democracy. One student, Melissa Jessup, started thinking about the assignment by brainstorming. First, she simply wrote down anything about life in a democracy that occurred to her:

voting rights	*welfare*	*freedom of press*
protest movements	*everybody equal*	*minorities*
racial prejudice	*American Dream*	*injustice*
the individual	*no job security*	*lobbyists and PACs*
justice takes time	*psychological factors*	*aristocracy of wealth*
size of bureaucracy		

Thinking through her list, Melissa decided to divide it into two separate lists: one devoted to positive aspects of life in a democracy; the other, to negative aspects. At this point she decided to discard some items that were redundant or did not seem to have much potential. As you can see, Melissa had some questions about where some of her items would fit:

POSITIVE	NEGATIVE
voting rights	*aristocracy of wealth*
freedom of the press	*justice takes time*
everybody equal	*racial prejudice*
American Dream	*welfare*
psychological factors	*lobbyists and PACs*
protest movements (positive?)	*size of bureaucracy*

At this point, Melissa decided that her topic would be about the ways in which money and special interests affect a democratically elected government. Which items on her lists would be relevant to her paper?

Asking Questions. It is always possible to ask most or all of the following questions about any topic: *Who? What? When? Where? Why? How?* They force you to approach the topic as a journalist does, setting it within different perspectives that can then be compared.

A professor asked her class on the judicial process to write a paper describing the impact of Supreme Court clerks on the decision-making process. One student developed the following questions as he began to think about a thesis:

Who are the Supreme Court's clerks? (How old? What is their racial and gender mix? What are their politics?)

What are their qualifications for the job?

What exactly is their job?

When during the court term are they most influential?

Where do they come from? (Is there any geographical or religious pattern in the way they are chosen? Do certain law schools contribute a significantly greater number of clerks than others?)

How are they chosen? (Are they appointed? elected?)

When in their careers do they serve?

Why are they chosen as they are?

Who have been some influential court clerks? (Have any gone on to sit on the bench themselves?)

Can you think of other questions that would make for useful inquiry?

Maintaining Flexibility. As you engage in invention strategies, you are also performing other writing tasks. You are still narrowing your topic, for example, as well as making decisions that will affect your choice of tone or audience. You are moving forward on all fronts with each decision you make affecting the others. This means that you must be flexible enough to allow for slight adjustments in your understanding of the paper's development and of your goal. Never be so determined to prove a particular theory that you fail to notice when your own understanding of it changes. Stay objective.

1.10   Organize Your Writing

A paper that contains all the necessary facts but presents them in an ineffective order will confuse rather than inform or persuade. Although there are various methods of grouping ideas, none is potentially more effective than outlining. Unfortunately, no organizing process is more often misunderstood.

Outlining for Yourself.   Outlining can do two jobs. First, it can force you, the writer, to gain a better understanding of your ideas by arranging them according to their interrelationships. There is one primary rule of outlining: ideas of equal weight are placed on the same level within the outline. This rule requires you to determine the relative importance of your ideas. You have to decide which ideas are of the same type or order, and into which subtopic each idea best fits.

If, in the planning stage, you carefully arrange your ideas in a coherent outline, your grasp of your topic will be greatly enhanced. You will have linked your ideas logically together and given a basic structure to the body of the paper. This sort of subordinating and coordinating activity is difficult, however, and as a result, inexperienced writers sometimes begin to write their first draft without an effective outline, hoping for the best. This hope is usually unfulfilled, especially in complex papers involving research.

EXERCISE 1.5   Organizing Thoughts

Rodrigo, a student in a second-year class in government management, researched the impact of a worker-retraining program in his state and came up with the following facts and theories. Number them in logical order:

____ A growing number of workers in the state do not possess the basic skills and education demanded by employers.

____ The number of dislocated workers in the state increased from 21,000 in 2001 to 32,000 in 2011.

____ A public policy to retrain uneducated workers would allow them to move into new and expanding sectors of the state economy.

____ Investment in high technology would allow the state's employers to remain competitive in the production of goods and services in both domestic and foreign markets.

____ The state's economy is becoming more global and more competitive.

Outlining for Your Reader.   The second job an outline can perform is to serve as a reader's blueprint to the paper, summarizing its points and their interrelationships. By consulting your outline, a busy policymaker can quickly get a sense of your paper's goal and the argument you have used to promote it. The clarity and coherence of the outline help determine how much attention your audience will give to your ideas.

As political science students, you will be given a great deal of help with the arrangement of your material into an outline to accompany your paper. A look at the formats presented in Chapter 4 of this manual will show you how strictly these formal outlines are structured. But, although you must pay close attention to these requirements, do not forget how powerful a tool an outline can be in the early planning stages of your paper.

The Formal Outline Pattern.   Following this pattern accurately during the planning stage of your paper helps to guarantee that your ideas are placed logically:

Thesis sentence (precedes the formal outline)

I. First main idea
   A. First subordinate idea
      1. Reason, example, or illustration
         a. Supporting detail
         b. Supporting detail
         c. Supporting detail
      2. Reason, example, or illustration
         a. Supporting detail
         b. Supporting detail
         c. Supporting detail
   B. Second subordinate idea
II. Second main idea

Notice that each level of the paper must have more than one entry; for every A there must be at least a B (and, if required, a C, a D, and so on), and for every 1 there must be a 2. This arrangement forces you to *compare ideas*, looking carefully at each one to determine its place among the others. The insistence on assigning relative values to your ideas is what makes an outline an effective organizing tool.

The Patterns of Political Science Papers.   The structure of any particular type of political science paper is governed by a formal pattern. When rigid external controls are placed on their writing, some writers feel that their creativity is hampered by a kind of "paint-by-numbers" approach to structure. It is vital to the success of your paper that you never allow yourself to be overwhelmed by the pattern rules for any type of paper. Remember that such controls exist not to limit your creativity but to make the paper immediately and easily useful to its intended audience. It is as necessary to write clearly and confidently in a position paper or a policy analysis paper as in a term paper for English literature, a résumé, a short story, or a job application letter.

1.11   Draft Your Writing

The Rough Draft.   After planning comes the writing of the first draft. Using your thesis and outline as direction markers, you must now weave your amalgam of ideas, data, and persuasion strategies into logically ordered sentences and paragraphs. Although adequate prewriting may facilitate drafting, it still will not be easy. Writers establish their own individual methods of encouraging themselves to forge ahead with the draft, but here are some tips:

1. Remember that this is a rough draft, not the final paper. At this stage, it is not necessary that every word be the best possible choice. Do not put that sort of pressure on yourself. You must not allow anything to slow you down now. Writing is not like sculpting in stone, where every chip is permanent; you can always go back to

your draft and add, delete, reword, and rearrange. *No matter how much effort you have put into planning, you cannot be sure how much of this first draft you will eventually keep.* It may take several drafts to get one that you find satisfactory.

2. Give yourself sufficient time to write. Do not delay the first draft by telling yourself there is still more research to do. You cannot uncover all the material there is to know on a particular subject, so do not fool yourself into trying. Remember that writing is a process of discovery. You may have to begin writing before you can see exactly what sort of research you need to do. Keep in mind that there are other tasks waiting for you after the first draft is finished, so allow for them as you determine your writing schedule.

More importantly, give yourself time to write, because the more time that passes after you have written a draft, the better your ability to view it with objectivity. It is very difficult to evaluate your writing accurately soon after you complete it. You need to cool down, to recover from the effort of putting all those words together. The "colder" you get on your writing, the better you are able to read it as if it were written by someone else and thus acknowledge the changes you will need to make to strengthen the paper.

3. Stay sharp. Keep in mind the plan you created as you narrowed your topic, composed a thesis sentence, and outlined the material. But, if you begin to feel a strong need to change the plan a bit, do not be afraid to do so. Be ready for surprises dealt you by your own growing understanding of your topic. Your goal is to record your best thinking on the subject as accurately as possible.

Paragraph Development.   There is no absolute requirement for the structure of any paragraph in your paper except that all its sentences must be clearly related to each other and each must carry the job of saying what you want to say about your thesis *one step farther.* In other words, any sentence that simply restates something said in another sentence anywhere else in the paper is a waste of your time and the reader's. It isn't unusual for a paragraph to have, somewhere in it, a *topic* sentence that serves as the key to the paragraph's organization and announces the paragraph's connection to the paper's thesis. But not all paragraphs need topic sentences.

What all paragraphs in the paper *do* need is an organizational strategy. Here are four typical organizational models, any one of which, if you keep it in mind, can help you build a coherent paragraph:

- *Chronological organization*: The sentences of the paragraph describe a series of events or steps or observations as they occur over time. This happens, then that, and then that.
- *Spatial organization*: The sentences of the paragraph record details of its subject in some logical order: top to bottom, up to down, outside to inside.
- *General-to-specific organization*: The paragraph starts with a statement of its main idea and then goes into detail as it discusses that idea.
- *Specific-to-general organization*: The paragraph begins with smaller, nuts-and-bolts details, arranging them into a larger pattern that, by the end of the paragraph, leads to the conclusion that is the paragraph's main idea.

These aren't the only organizational strategies available to you, and, of course, different paragraphs in a paper can use different strategies, though a paragraph that employs more than one organizational plan is risking incoherence. The essential thing to remember is that each sentence in the paragraph must bear a logical relationship to the one before it and the one after it. It is this notion of *interconnectedness* that can prevent you from getting off track and stuffing extraneous material in your paragraphs.

Like all other aspects of the writing process, paragraph development is a challenge. But remember, one of the helpful facts about paragraphs is that they are relatively small, especially compared to the overall scope of your paper. Each paragraph can basically do only one job—handle or help to handle a single idea, which is itself only a part of the overall development of the larger thesis idea. That paragraphs are small and aimed at a single task means that it is relatively easy to revise them. By focusing clearly on the single job a paragraph does and filtering out all the paper's other claims for your attention, you should gain enough clarity of vision during the revision process to understand what you need to do to make that paragraph work better.

Authority.   To be convincing, your writing has to be authoritative; that is, you have to sound as if you have complete confidence in your ability to convey your ideas in words. Sentences that sound stilted, or that suffer from weak phrasing or the use of clichés, are not going to win supporters for the positions that you express in your paper. So a major question becomes, "How can I sound confident?"

Here are some points to consider as you work to convey to your reader that necessary sense of authority:

Level of Formality.   Tone is one of the primary methods by which you signal to the readers who you are and what your attitude is toward them and toward your topic. Your major decision is which level of language formality is most appropriate to your audience. The informal tone you would use in a letter to a friend might well be out of place in a paper on "Waste in Military Spending" written for your government professor. Remember that tone is only part of the overall decision that you make about how to present your information. Formality is, to some extent, a function of individual word choices and phrasing. For example, is it appropriate to use contractions such as *isn't* or *they'll*? Would the strategic use of a sentence fragment for effect be out of place? The use of informal language, the personal *I*, and the second-person *you* is traditionally forbidden—for better or worse—in certain kinds of writing. Often, part of the challenge of writing a formal paper is simply how to give your prose impact while staying within the conventions.

Jargon.   One way to lose readers quickly is to overwhelm them with *jargon*—phrases that have a special, usually technical meaning within your discipline but that are unfamiliar to the average reader. The very occasional use of jargon may add an effective touch of atmosphere, but anything more than that will severely dampen a reader's enthusiasm for the paper. Often the writer uses jargon in an effort to impress the reader by sounding lofty or knowledgeable. Unfortunately, all jargon usually does is cause confusion. In fact, the use of jargon indicates a writer's lack of connection to the audience.

Political science writing is a haven for jargon. Perhaps writers of policy analyses and position papers believe their readers are all completely attuned to their terminology. Or some may hope to obscure damaging information or potentially unpopular ideas in confusing language. In other cases, the problem could simply be unclear thinking by the writer. Whatever the reason, the fact is that political science papers too often sound like prose made by machines to be read by machines.

Some students may feel that, to be accepted as political scientists, their papers should conform to the practices of their published peers. This is a mistake. Remember that it is never better to write a cluttered or confusing sentence than a clear one, and burying your ideas in jargon defeats the effort that you went through to form them.

EXERCISE 1.6   Revising Jargon

What words in the following sentence, from an article in a political science journal, are jargon? Can you rewrite it to clarify its meaning?

> The implementation of statute-mandated regulated inputs exceeds the conceptualization of the administrative technicians.

Clichés.   In the heat of composition, as you are looking for words to help you form your ideas, it is sometimes easy to plug in a *cliché*—a phrase that has attained universal recognition by overuse. (*Note:* Clichés differ from jargon in that clichés are part of the general public's everyday language, whereas jargon is specific to the language of experts in a field.) Our vocabularies are brimming with clichés:

It's raining cats and dogs.

That issue is as dead as a doornail.

It's time for the governor to face the music.

Angry voters made a beeline for the ballot box.

The problem with clichés is that they are virtually meaningless. Once colorful means of expression, they have lost their color through overuse, and they tend to bleed energy and color from the surrounding words. When revising, replace clichés with fresh wording that more accurately conveys your point.

Descriptive Language.   Language that appeals to readers' senses will always engage their interest more fully than language that is abstract. This is especially important for writing in disciplines that tend to deal in abstracts, such as political science. The typical political science paper, with its discussions of principles, demographics, or points of law, is usually in danger of floating off into abstraction, with each paragraph drifting further away from the felt life of the readers. Whenever appropriate, appeal to your readers' sense of sight, hearing, taste, touch, or smell.

EXERCISE 1.7   Using Descriptive Language

Which of these two sentences is more effective?

1. The housing project had deteriorated badly since the last inspection.
2. The housing project had deteriorated badly since the last inspection; stench rose from the plumbing, grime coated the walls and floors, and rats scurried through the hallways.

Bias-Free and Gender-Neutral Writing.   Language can be a very powerful method of either reinforcing or destroying cultural stereotypes. By treating the sexes in subtly different ways in your language, you may unknowingly be committing an act of discrimination. A common example is the use of the pronoun *he* to refer to a person whose gender has not been identified.

Some writers, faced with this dilemma, alternate the use of male and female personal pronouns; others use the plural to avoid the need to use a pronoun of either gender:

Sexist: A lawyer should always treat his client with respect.

Corrected: A lawyer should always treat his or her client with respect.

Or: Lawyers should always treat their clients with respect.

Sexist: Man is a political animal.

Corrected: People are political animals.

Remember that language is more than the mere vehicle of your thoughts. Your words shape perceptions for your readers. How well you say something will profoundly affect your readers' response to what you say. Sexist language denies to a large number of your readers the basic right to fair and equal treatment. Make sure your writing is not guilty of this form of discrimination.

Revising.   After all the work you have gone through writing it, you may feel "married" to the first draft of your paper. However, revision is one of the most important steps in ensuring your paper's success. Although unpracticed writers often think of revision as little more than making sure all the *i*'s are dotted and *t*'s are crossed, it is much more than that. Revising is *reseeing* the essay, looking at it from other perspectives, trying always to align your view with the one that will be held by your audience. Research indicates that we are actually revising all the time, in every phase of the writing process, as we reread phrases, rethink the placement of an item in an outline, or test a new topic sentence for a paragraph. Subjecting your entire hard-fought draft to cold, objective scrutiny is one of the toughest activities to master, but it is absolutely necessary. You have to make sure that you have said everything that needs to be said clearly and logically. One confusing passage will deflect the reader's attention from where you want it to be. Suddenly the reader has to become a detective, trying to figure out why you wrote, what you did, and what you meant by it. You do not want to throw such obstacles in the path of understanding.

Here are some tips to help you with revision:

1. Give yourself adequate time for revision. As discussed above, you need time to become "cold" on your paper in order to analyze it objectively. After you have written your draft, spend some time away from it. Then try to reread it as if someone else had written it.

2. Read the paper carefully. This is tougher than it sounds. One good strategy is to read it aloud yourself or to have a friend read it aloud while you listen. (Note, however, that friends are usually not the best critics. They are rarely trained in revision techniques and are often unwilling to risk disappointing you by giving your paper a really thorough examination.)

3. Have a list of specific items to check. It is important to revise in an orderly fashion, in stages, first looking at large concerns, such as the overall organization, and then at smaller elements, such as paragraph or sentence structure.

4. Check for unity—the clear and logical relation of all parts of the essay to its thesis. Make sure that every paragraph relates well to the whole of the paper and is in the right place.

5. Check for coherence. Make sure there are no gaps between the various parts of the argument. Look to see that you have adequate transitions everywhere they are needed. Transitional elements are markers indicating places where the paper's focus or attitude changes. Such elements can take the form of one word—*however, although, unfortunately, luckily*—or an entire sentence or a paragraph: *In order to fully appreciate the importance of democracy as a shaping presence in post–Cold War Polish politics, it is necessary to examine briefly the Poles' last historical attempt to implement democratic government.*

Transitional elements rarely introduce new material. Instead, they are direction pointers, either indicating a shift to new subject matter or signaling how the writer wishes certain material to be interpreted by the reader. Because you, the writer, already know where and why your paper changes direction and how you want particular passages to be received, it can be very difficult for you to catch those places where transition is needed.

6. Avoid unnecessary repetition. Two types of repetition can annoy a reader: repetition of content and repetition of wording.

Repetition of content occurs when you return to a subject you have already discussed. Ideally, you should deal with a topic once, memorably, and then move on to your next subject. Organizing a paper is a difficult task, however, which usually occurs through a process of enlightenment in terms of purposes and strategies, and repetition of content can happen even if you have used prewriting strategies. What is worse, it can be difficult for you to be aware of the repetition in your own writing. As you write and revise, remember that any unnecessary repetition of content in your final draft is potentially annoying to your readers, who are working to make sense of the argument they are reading and do not want to be distracted by a passage repeating material they have already encountered. You must train yourself, through practice, to look for material that you have repeated unnecessarily.

Repetition of wording occurs when you overuse certain phrases or words. This can make your prose sound choppy and uninspired, as the following examples demonstrate:

> The subcommittee's report on education reform will surprise a number of people. A number of people will want copies of the report.

> The chairman said at a press conference that he is happy with the report. He will circulate it to the local news agencies in the morning. He will also make sure that the city council has copies.

> I became upset when I heard how the committee had voted. I called the chairman and expressed my reservations about the committee's decision. I told him I felt that he had let the teachers and students of the state down. I also issued a press statement.

The last passage illustrates a condition known by composition teachers as the *I-syndrome*. Can you hear how such duplicated phrasing can hurt a paper? Your language should sound fresh and energetic. Make sure, before you submit your final draft, to read through your paper carefully, looking for such repetition. However, not all repetition is bad. You may wish to repeat a phrase for rhetorical effect or special emphasis: "I came. I saw. I conquered." Just make sure that any repetition in your paper is intentional, placed there to produce a specific effect.

Editing.   Editing is sometimes confused with the more involved process of revising. But editing is done later in the writing process, after you have wrestled through your first draft—and maybe your second and third—and arrived at the final draft. Even though your draft now contains all the information you want to impart and has the information arranged to your satisfaction, there are still many factors to check, such as sentence structure, spelling, and punctuation.

It is at this point that an unpracticed writer might be less than vigilant. After all, most of the work on the paper is finished, as the "big jobs" of discovering, organizing, and drafting information have been completed. But watch out! Editing is as important as any other part of the writing process. Any error that you allow in the final draft will count against you in the mind of the reader. This may not seem fair, but even a minor error—a misspelling or confusing placement of a comma—will make a much greater impression on your reader than perhaps it should. Remember that everything about your paper is your responsibility, including performing even the supposedly little jobs correctly. Careless editing undermines the effectiveness of your paper. It would be a shame if all the hard work you put into prewriting, drafting, and revising were to be damaged because you carelessly allowed a comma splice!

Most of the tips given above for revising hold for editing as well. It is best to edit in stages, looking for only one or two kinds of errors each time you reread the paper. Focus especially on errors that you remember committing in the past. If, for instance, you know that you have a tendency to misplace commas, go through your paper looking at each comma carefully. If you have a weakness for writing unintentional sentence fragments, read each sentence aloud to make sure that it is indeed a complete sentence. Have you accidentally shifted verb tenses anywhere, moving from past to present tense for no reason? Do all the subjects in your sentences agree in number with their verbs? *Now is the time to find out.*

Watch out for *miscues*—problems with a sentence that the writer simply does not see. Remember that your search for errors is hampered in two ways:

1. As the writer, you hope not to find any errors in your work. This desire can cause you to miss mistakes when they do occur.
2. Because you know your material so well, it is easy, as you read, to unconsciously supply missing material—a word, a piece of punctuation—as if it were present.

How difficult is it to see that something is missing in the following sentence? Unfortunately, legislators often have too little regard their constituents.

We can guess that the missing word is probably *for,* which should be inserted after *regard.* It is quite possible, however, that the writer of the sentence would automatically supply the missing *for* as if it were on the page. This is a miscue, which can be hard for writers to spot because they are so close to their material.

One tactic for catching mistakes in sentence structure is to read the sentences aloud, starting with the last one in the paper and then moving to the next-to-last, then to the previous sentence, and thus going backward through the paper (reading each sentence in the normal, left-to-right manner, of course) until you reach the first sentence of the introduction. This backward progression strips each sentence of its rhetorical context and helps you focus on its internal structure.

Editing is the stage in which you finally answer those minor questions that you had put off when you were wrestling with wording and organization. Any ambiguities regarding the use of abbreviations, italics, numerals, capital letters, titles (When do you capitalize the title *president,* for example?), hyphens, dashes (usually created on a typewriter or computer by striking the hyphen key twice), apostrophes, and quotation marks have to be cleared up now. You must also check to see that you have used the required formats for footnotes, endnotes, margins, page numbers, and the like.

Guessing is not allowed. Sometimes unpracticed writers who realize that they do not quite understand a particular rule of grammar, punctuation, or format do nothing to fill that knowledge gap. Instead they rely on guesswork and their own logic—which is not always up to the task of dealing with so contrary a language as English—to get them through problems that they could solve if they referred to a writing manual. Remember that it does not matter to the reader why or how an error shows up in your writing. It only matters that you have dropped your guard. You must not allow a careless error to undo all the good work that you have done.

Proofreading. Before you hand in the final version of your paper, it is vital that you check it one more time to make sure there are no errors of any sort. This job is called *proofreading*, or *proofing*. In essence, you are looking for many of the same things you had checked for during editing, but now you are doing it on the last draft, which is about to be submitted to your audience. Proofreading is as important as editing; you may have missed an error that you still have time to find, or an error may have been introduced when the draft was recopied or typed for the last time. Like every other stage of the writing process, proofreading is your responsibility.

At this point, you must check for typing mistakes: transposed or deleted letters, words, phrases, or punctuation. If you have had the paper professionally typed, you still must check it carefully. Do not rely solely on the typist's proofreading. If you are creating your paper on a computer or a word processor, it is possible for you to un-intentionally insert a command that alters your document drastically by slicing out a word, line, or sentence at the touch of a key. Make sure such accidental deletions have not occurred.

Above all else, remember that your paper represents you. It is a product of your best thinking, your most energetic and imaginative response to a writing challenge. If you have maintained your enthusiasm for the project and worked through the stages of the writing process honestly and carefully, you should produce a paper you can be proud of, one that will serve its readers well.

CHAPTER 2

Master the Basics of Language and Scholarship

2.1   Avoid Errors in Grammar and Punctuation

As various composition theorists have pointed out, the word *grammar* has several definitions. One meaning is "the formal patterns in which words must be arranged in order to convey meaning." We learn these patterns very early in life and use them spontaneously, without thinking. Our understanding of grammatical patterns is extremely sophisticated, despite the fact that few of us can actually cite the rules by which the patterns work. Patrick Hartwell tested grammar learning by asking native English speakers of different ages and levels of education, including high school teachers, to arrange these words in natural order:

French   the   young   girls   four

Everyone could produce the natural order for this phrase: "the four young French girls." Yet none of Hartwell's respondents said they knew the rule that governs the order of the words (Hartwell 1985, 111).

Eliminate Chronic Errors.   If just thinking about our errors has a negative effect on our writing, how do we learn to write more correctly? Perhaps the best answer is simply to write as often as possible. Give yourself lots of practice in putting your thoughts into written shape—and then in revising and proofing your work. As you write and revise, be honest with yourself—and patient. Chronic errors are like bad habits; getting rid of them takes time.

You probably know of one or two problem areas in your writing that you could have eliminated but have not. Instead, you may have "fudged" your writing at the critical points, relying on half-remembered formulas from past English classes or trying to come up with logical solutions to your writing problems. (*Warning:* The English language does not always work in a way that seems logical.) You may have simply decided that comma rules are unlearnable or that you will never understand the difference between the verbs *lay* and *lie*. And so you guess, and you come up with the wrong answer a good part of the time. What a shame, when just a little extra work would give you mastery over those few gaps in your understanding and boost your confidence as well.

Instead of continuing with this sort of guesswork and living with the holes in your knowledge, why not face the problem areas now and learn the rules that have heretofore escaped you? What follows is a discussion of those surface features of writing in which errors most commonly occur. You will probably be familiar with most if not all of the rules discussed, but there may well be a few you have not yet mastered. Now is the time to do so.

2.2   Apostrophes

An apostrophe is used to show possession. When you wish to say that something belongs to someone or something, you add either an apostrophe and an *s* or an apostrophe alone to the word that represents the owner.

- **When the owner is singular** (a single person or thing), the apostrophe precedes an added *s*:

     According to Mayor Anderson's secretary, the news broadcast has been canceled.

     The union's lawyers challenged the government's policy in court.

     Somebody's briefcase was left in the auditorium.

- The same rule applies **if the owner is a plural that does not end in *s*:**

     The women's club sponsored several debates during the last presidential campaign.

     Governor Smith has proven himself a tireless worker for children's rights.

- **When the owner is a plural ending in *s*,** the apostrophe follows the *s*:

     The new legislation was discussed at the secretaries' conference.

- There are two ways **to form the possessive for two or more nouns:**

  1. To show joint possession (both nouns owning the same thing or things), the last noun in the series is possessive:

     The president and first lady's invitations were sent out yesterday.

  2. To indicate that each noun owns an item or items individually, each noun must show possession:

     Mayor Scott's and Mayor MacKay's speeches took different approaches to the same problem.

The importance of the apostrophe is obvious when you consider the difference in meaning between the following two sentences:

Be sure to pick up the senator's bags on your way to the airport.

Be sure to pick up the senators' bags on your way to the airport.

In the first sentence, you have only one senator to worry about, whereas in the second, you have at least two!

A Prepostrophe?   James Swanson, political commentator and editor of the *Gesundheit Gazette*, occasionally encounters political statements that he finds to be preposterous. He believes that journalists should warn us when they print one of these statements by placing a "prepostrophe" ∧ at the end of a preposterous sentence. Consider, for example, how a prepostrophe might assist the reader in the following statement: "We can cut taxes without reducing services ∧" For even more preposterous statements, we add more prepostrophes: "Iraq has weapons of mass destruction ∧ ∧"

2.3   Capitalization

Here is a brief summary of some hard-to-remember capitalization rules:

1. You may, if you choose, capitalize the first letter of the first word in a sentence that follows a colon. However, make sure you use one pattern consistently throughout your paper:

   > Our instructions are explicit: *Do not* allow anyone into the conference without an identification badge.

   > Our instructions are explicit: *do not* allow anyone into the conference without an identification badge.

2. Capitalize *proper nouns* (names of specific people, places, or things) and *proper adjectives* (adjectives made from proper nouns). A common noun following a proper adjective is usually not capitalized, nor is a common adjective preceding a proper adjective (such as *a, an,* or *the*):

PROPER NOUNS	PROPER ADJECTIVES
Poland	Polish officials
Iraq	the Iraqi ambassador
Shakespeare	a Shakespearean tragedy

Proper nouns include:

- *Names of monuments and buildings:* the Washington Monument, the Empire State Building, the Library of Congress
- *Historical events, eras, and certain terms concerning calendar dates:* the Civil War, the Dark Ages, Monday, December, Columbus Day
- *Parts of the country:* North, Southwest, Eastern Seaboard, the West Coast, New England.

- **Note:** When words like *north, south, east, west,* and *northwest* are used to designate direction rather than geographical region, they are not capitalized: "We drove east to Boston and then made a tour of the East Coast."

- *Words referring to race, religion, and nationality:* Islam, Muslim, Caucasian, White (or white), Asian, Negro, Black (or black), Slavic, Arab, Jewish, Hebrew, Buddhism, Buddhists, Southern Baptists, the Bible, the Koran, American

- *Names of languages:* English, Chinese, Latin, Sanskrit
- *Titles of corporations, institutions, universities, and organizations:* Dow Chemical, General Motors, the National Endowment for the Humanities, University of Tennessee, Colby College, Kiwanis Club, American Association of Retired Persons, Oklahoma State Senate

---

■ **Note:** Some words once considered proper nouns or adjectives have, over time, become common and are no longer capitalized, such as *french fries, pasteurized milk, arabic numerals,* and *italics.*

---

3. Titles of individuals may be capitalized if they precede a proper name; otherwise, titles are usually not capitalized:

> The committee honored Senator Jones.
> The committee honored the senator from Kansas.
> We phoned Doctor Jessup, who arrived shortly afterward.
> We phoned the doctor, who arrived shortly afterward.
> A story on Queen Elizabeth's health appeared in yesterday's paper.
> A story on the queen's health appeared in yesterday's paper.
> Pope John Paul's visit to Colorado was a public relations success.
> The pope's visit to Colorado was a public relations success.

When Not to Capitalize

In general, you do not capitalize nouns when your reference is nonspecific. For example, you would not capitalize *the senator,* but you would capitalize *Senator Smith.* The second reference is as much a title as it is a term of identification, whereas the first reference is a mere identifier. Likewise, there is a difference in degree of specificity between *the state treasury* and *the Texas State Treasury.*

■ **Note:** The meaning of a term may change somewhat depending on its capitalization. What, for example, might be the difference between a *Democrat* and a *democrat?* When capitalized, the word refers to a member of a specific political party; when not capitalized, it refers to someone who believes in the democratic form of government.

Capitalization depends to some extent on the context of your writing. For example, if you are writing a policy analysis for a specific corporation, you may capitalize words and phrases that refer to that corporation—such as *Board of Directors, Chairman of the Board,* and *the Institute*—that would not be capitalized in a paper written for a more general audience. Likewise, in some contexts, it is not unusual to see the titles of certain powerful officials capitalized even when not accompanying a proper noun:

> The President took few members of his staff to Camp David with him.

2.4   Colons

We all know certain uses for the colon. A colon can, for example, separate the parts of a statement of time (*4:25 A.M.*), separate chapter and verse in a biblical quotation (*John 3:16*), and close the salutation of a business letter (*Dear Senator Keaton:*). But the colon has other, less well-known uses that can add extra flexibility to sentence structure.

The colon can introduce into a sentence certain kinds of material, such as a list, a quotation, or a restatement or description of material mentioned earlier:

List

The committee's research proposal promised to do three things: (1) establish the extent of the problem, (2) examine several possible solutions, and (3) estimate the cost of each solution.

Quotation

In his speech, the mayor challenged us with these words: "How will your council's work make a difference in the life of our city?"

Restatement or Description

Ahead of us, according to the senator's chief of staff, lay the biggest job of all: convincing our constituents of the plan's benefits.

2.5   Commas

The comma is perhaps the most troublesome of all marks of punctuation, no doubt because its use is governed by so many variables, such as sentence length, rhetorical emphasis, and changing notions of style. The most common problems are outlined below.

The Comma Splice

A *comma splice* is the joining of two complete sentences with only a comma:

An impeachment is merely an indictment of a government official, actual removal usually requires a vote by a legislative body.

An unemployed worker who has been effectively retrained is no longer an economic problem for the community, he has become an asset.

It might be possible for the city to assess fees on the sale of real estate, however, such a move would be criticized by the community of real estate developers.

In each of these passages, two complete sentences (also called *independent clauses*) have been spliced together by a comma, which is an inadequate break between the two sentences.

One foolproof way to check your paper for comma splices is to read the structures on both sides of each comma carefully. If you find a complete sentence on each side, and if the sentence following the comma does not begin with a coordinating conjunction (*and, but, for, nor, or, so, yet*), then you have found a comma splice.

Simply reading the draft to try to "hear" the comma splices may not work because the rhetorical features of your prose—its "movement"—may make it hard to detect this kind of error in sentence completeness. There are five commonly used ways to correct comma splices:

1. Place a period between the two independent clauses:

INCORRECT   A political candidate receives many benefits from his or her affiliation with a political party, there are liabilities as well.

CORRECT   A political candidate receives many benefits from his or her affiliation with a political party. There are liabilities as well.

2. Place a comma and a coordinating conjunction (*and, but, for, or, nor, so, yet*) between the independent clauses:

INCORRECT   The councilman's speech described the major differences of opinion over the economic situation, it also suggested a possible course of action.

CORRECT   The councilman's speech described the major differences of opinion over the economic situation, and it also suggested a possible course of action.

3. Place a semicolon between the independent clauses:

INCORRECT   Some people feel that the federal government should play a large role in establishing a housing policy for the homeless, many others disagree.

CORRECT   Some people feel that the federal government should play a large role in establishing a housing policy for the homeless; many others disagree.

4. Rewrite the two clauses as one independent clause:

INCORRECT   Television ads played a big part in the campaign, however they were not the deciding factor in the challenger's victory over the incumbent.

CORRECT   Television ads played a large but not a decisive role in the challenger's victory over the incumbent.

5. Change one of the independent clauses into a dependent clause by beginning it with a subordinating word (*although, after, as, because, before, if, though,*

unless, when, which, where), which prevents the clause from being able to stand on its own as a complete sentence.

INCORRECT   The election was held last Tuesday, there was a poor voter turnout.

CORRECT   When the election was held last Tuesday, there was a poor voter turnout.

Commas in a Compound Sentence

A *compound sentence* is composed of two or more independent clauses—two complete sentences. When these two clauses are joined by a coordinating conjunction, the conjunction should be preceded by a comma to signal the reader that another independent clause follows. (This is method number 2 for fixing a comma splice, described above.) When the comma is missing, the reader is not expecting to find the second half of a compound sentence and may be distracted from the text.

As the following examples indicate, the missing comma is especially a problem in longer sentences or in sentences in which other coordinating conjunctions appear. Notice how the comma sorts out the two main parts of the compound sentence, eliminating confusion:

INCORRECT   The senator promised to visit the hospital and investigate the problem and then he called the press conference to a close.

CORRECT   The senator promised to visit the hospital and investigate the problem, and then he called the press conference to a close.

INCORRECT   The water board can neither make policy nor enforce it nor can its members serve on auxiliary water committees.

CORRECT   The water board can neither make policy nor enforce it, nor can its members serve on auxiliary water committees.

An exception to this rule arises in shorter sentences, where the comma may not be necessary to make the meaning clear:

The mayor phoned and we thanked him for his support.

However, it is never wrong to place a comma after the conjunction between independent clauses. If you are the least bit unsure of your audience's notion of "proper" grammar, it is a good idea to take the conservative approach and use the comma:

The mayor phoned, and we thanked him for his support.

Commas with Restrictive and Nonrestrictive Elements

A *nonrestrictive element* is a part of a sentence—a word, phrase, or clause—that adds information about another element in the sentence without restricting or limiting its meaning. Although this information may be useful, the nonrestrictive element is not needed for the sentence to make sense. To signal its inessential nature, the nonrestrictive element is set off from the rest of the sentence with commas.

The failure to use commas to indicate the nonrestrictive nature of a sentence element can cause confusion. See, for example, how the presence or absence of commas affects our understanding of the following sentence:

> The mayor was talking with the policeman, who won the outstanding service award last year.

> The mayor was talking with the policeman who won the outstanding service award last year.

Can you see that the comma changes the meaning of the sentence? In the first version of the sentence, the comma makes the information that follows it incidental: *The mayor was talking with the policeman, who happens to have won the service award last year.* In the second version of the sentence, the information following the word *policeman* is vital to the sense of the sentence; it tells us specifically *which* policeman— presumably there are more than one—the mayor was addressing. Here, the lack of a comma has transformed the material following the word *policeman* into a *restrictive element*, which means that it is necessary to our understanding of the sentence.

Be sure that you make a clear distinction in your paper between nonrestrictive and restrictive elements by setting off the nonrestrictive elements with commas.

Commas in a Series

A series is any two or more items of a similar nature that appear consecutively in a sentence. These items may be individual words, phrases, or clauses. In a series of three or more items, the items are separated by commas:

> The senator, the mayor, and the police chief all attended the ceremony.

> Because of the new zoning regulations, all trailer parks must be moved out of the neighborhood, all small businesses must apply for recertification and tax status, and the two local churches must repave their parking lots.

The final comma in the series, the one before *and*, is sometimes left out, especially in newspaper writing. This practice, however, can make for confusion, especially in longer, complicated sentences like the second example above. Here is the way this sentence would read without the final, or serial, comma:

> Because of the new zoning regulations, all trailer parks must be moved out of the neighborhood, all small businesses must apply for recertification and tax status and the two local churches must repave their parking lots.

Notice that, without a comma, the division between the second and third items in the series is not clear. This is the sort of ambiguous structure that can cause a reader to backtrack and lose concentration. You can avoid such confusion by always using that final comma. Remember, however, that if you do decide to include it, do so consistently; make sure it appears in every series in your paper.

2.6   Modifiers

A *modifier* is a word or group of words used to describe, or modify, another word in the sentence. A *misplaced modifier*, sometimes called a dangling modifier, appears at either the beginning or the end of a sentence and seems to be describing some word other than the one the writer obviously intended. The modifier therefore "dangles," disconnected from its correct meaning. It is often hard for the writer to spot a dangling modifier, but readers can—and will—find them, and the result can be disastrous for the sentence, as the following examples demonstrate:

INCORRECT   Flying low over Washington, the White House was seen.

CORRECT   Flying low over Washington, we saw the White House.

INCORRECT   Worried at the cost of the program, sections of the bill were trimmed in committee.

CORRECT   Worried at the cost of the program, the committee trimmed sections of the bill.

INCORRECT   To lobby for prison reform, a lot of effort went into the television ads.

CORRECT   The lobby group put a lot of effort into the television ads advocating prison reform.

INCORRECT   Stunned, the television broadcast the defeated senator's concession speech.

CORRECT   The television broadcast the stunned senator's concession speech.

Note that, in the first two incorrect sentences above, the confusion is largely due to the use of *passive-voice* verbs: "the White House *was seen*," "sections of the bill *were trimmed*." Often, although not always, a dangling modifier results because the actor in the sentence—*we* in the first sentence, *the committee* in the second—is either distanced from the modifier or obliterated by the passive-voice verb. It is a good idea to avoid using the passive voice unless you have a specific reason for doing so.

One way to check for dangling modifiers is to examine all modifiers at the beginning or end of your sentences. Look especially for to be phrases or for words ending in *-ing* or *-ed* at the start of the modifier. Then see if the modified word is close enough to the phrase to be properly connected.

2.7   Parallelism

Series of two or more words, phrases, or clauses within a sentence should have the same grammatical structure, a situation called *parallelism*. Parallel structures can add power and balance to your writing by creating a strong rhetorical rhythm. Here is a famous example of parallelism from the Preamble to the U.S. Constitution. (The capitalization follows that of the original eighteenth-century document. Parallel structures have been italicized:)

> We the People of the United States, in Order to *form a more perfect Union, Establish justice, insure Domestic Tranquillity, provide for the common defense, promote the general Welfare,* and *secure the Blessings of Liberty to ourselves and our Posterity,* do *ordain* and *establish* this Constitution for the United States of America.

There are actually two series in this sentence: the first, composed of six phrases, each of which completes the infinitive phrase beginning with the word to [*to form*, (*to*) *Establish*, (*to*) *insure*, (*to*) *provide*, (*to*) *promote*, and (*to*) *secure*]; the second, consisting of two verbs (*ordain* and *establish*). These parallel series appeal to our love of balance and pattern, and give an authoritative tone to the sentence. The writer, we feel, has thought long and carefully about the matter at hand and has taken firm control of it.

Because we find a special satisfaction in balanced structures, we are more likely to remember ideas phrased in parallelisms than in less highly ordered language. For this reason, as well as for the sense of authority and control that they suggest, parallel structures are common in political utterances:

> *We hold these truths to be self-evident, that all men are created equal, that they are endowed by their Creator with certain unalienable rights, that among these are life, liberty, and the pursuit of happiness.*

—The Declaration of Independence, 1776

> *But in a larger sense, we cannot dedicate, we cannot consecrate, we cannot hallow this ground. The brave men, living and dead, who struggled here, have consecrated it far above our poor power to add or detract. The world will little note, nor long remember what we say here; but it can never forget what they did here.*

—Abraham Lincoln, **Gettysburg Address**, 1863

> *Ask not what your country can do for you, ask what you can do for your country.*

—John F. Kennedy, Inaugural Address, 1961

Faulty Parallelism

If the parallelism of a passage is not carefully maintained, the writing can seem sloppy and out of balance. Scan your writing to make sure that all series and lists have parallel structures. The following examples show how to correct faulty parallelism:

INCORRECT	The mayor promises not only *to reform* the police department but also *the giving of raises* to all city employees. (Connective structures such as *not only . . . but also* and *both . . . and* introduce elements that should be parallel.)
CORRECT	The mayor promises not only *to reform* the police department but also *to give* raises to all city employees.
INCORRECT	The cost *of doing nothing* is greater than the cost *to renovate* the apartment block.
CORRECT	The cost *of doing nothing* is greater than the cost *of renovating* the apartment block.

| INCORRECT | Here are the items on the committee's agenda: (1) *to discuss* the new property tax; (2) *to revise* the wording of the city charter; (3) *a vote* on the city manager's request for an assistant. |
| CORRECT | Here are the items on the committee's agenda: (1) *to discuss* the new property tax; (2) *to revise* the wording of the city charter; (3) *to vote* on the city manager's request for an assistant. |

2.8   Fused (Run-On) Sentences

A *fused sentence* is one in which two or more independent clauses (passages that can stand as complete sentences) have been run together without the aid of any suitable connecting word, phrase, or punctuation. There are several ways to correct a fused sentence:

INCORRECT	The council members were exhausted they had debated for two hours.
CORRECT	The council members were exhausted. They had debated for two hours. (The clauses have been separated into two sentences.)
CORRECT	The council members were exhausted; they had debated for two hours. (The clauses have been separated by a semicolon.)
CORRECT	The council members were exhausted, having debated for two hours. (The second clause has been rephrased as a dependent clause.)
INCORRECT	Our policy analysis impressed the committee it also convinced them to reconsider their action.
CORRECT	Our policy analysis impressed the committee and also convinced them to reconsider their action. (The second clause has been rephrased as part of the first clause.)
CORRECT	Our policy analysis impressed the committee, and it also convinced them to reconsider their action. (The clauses have been separated by a comma and a coordinating word.)

Although a fused sentence is easily noticeable to the reader, it can be maddeningly difficult for the writer to catch. Unpracticed writers tend to read through the fused spots, sometimes supplying the break that is usually heard when sentences are spoken. To check for fused sentences, read the independent clauses in your paper carefully, making sure that there are adequate breaks among all of them.

2.9   Pronouns

Its Versus *It's*

Do not make the mistake of trying to form the possessive of *it* in the same way that you form the possessive of most nouns. The pronoun *it* shows possession by simply adding an *s*.

> The prosecuting attorney argued the case on its merits.

The word *it's* is a contraction of *it is*:

> It's the most expensive program ever launched by the council.

What makes the *its/it's* rule so confusing is that most nouns form the singular possessive by adding an apostrophe and an *s:*

> The jury's verdict startled the crowd.

When proofreading, any time you come to the word *it's*, substitute the phrase *it is* while you read. If the phrase makes sense, you have used the correct form. If you have used the word *it's*:

> The newspaper article was misleading in *it's* analysis of the election.

Then read it as *it is*:

> The newspaper article was misleading in *it is* analysis of the election.

If the phrase makes no sense, substitute *its* for *it's*:

> The newspaper article was misleading in *its* analysis of the election.

Vague Pronoun References

Pronouns are words that take the place of nouns or other pronouns that have already been mentioned in your writing. The most common pronouns include *he, she, it, they, them, those, which,* and *who*. You must make sure there is no confusion about the word to which each pronoun refers:

> The mayor said that he would support our bill if the city council would also back it.

The word that the pronoun replaces is called its *antecedent*. To check the accuracy of your pronoun references, ask yourself, "To what does the pronoun refer?" Then answer the question carefully, making sure that there is not more than one possible antecedent. Consider the following example:

> Several special interest groups decided to defeat the new health care bill. This became the turning point of the government's reform campaign.

To what does the word *this* refer? The immediate answer seems to be the word *bill* at the end of the previous sentence. It is more likely that the writer was referring to the attempt of the special interest groups to defeat the bill, but there is no word in the first sentence that refers specifically to this action. The pronoun reference is thus unclear. One way to clarify the reference is to change the beginning of the second sentence:

> Several special interest groups decided to defeat the new health care bill. Their attack on the bill became the turning point of the government's reform campaign.

Here is another example:

> When John F. Kennedy appointed his brother Robert to the position of U.S. attorney general, he had little idea how widespread the corruption in the Teamsters Union was.

To whom does the word *he* refer? It is unclear whether the writer is referring to John or Robert Kennedy. One way to clarify the reference is simply to repeat the antecedent instead of using a pronoun:

> When John F. Kennedy appointed his brother Robert to the position of U.S. attorney general, Robert had little idea how widespread the corruption in the Teamsters Union was.

Pronoun Agreement

A pronoun must agree with its antecedent in both gender and number, as the following examples demonstrate:

> Mayor Smith said that he appreciated our club's support in the election.
>
> One reporter asked the senator what she would do if the president offered her a cabinet post.
>
> Having listened to our case, the judge decided to rule on it within the week.
>
> Engineers working on the housing project said they were pleased with the renovation so far.

Certain words, however, can be troublesome antecedents because they may look like plural pronouns but are actually singular:

anyone	each	either	everybody	everyone
nobody	no one	somebody	someone	

A pronoun referring to one of these words in a sentence must be singular too:

INCORRECT	Each of the women in the support group brought their children.
CORRECT	Each of the women in the support group brought her children.
INCORRECT	Has everybody received their ballot?
CORRECT	Has everybody received his or her ballot? (The two gender-specific pronouns are used to avoid sexist language.)
CORRECT	Have all the delegates received their ballots? (The singular antecedent has been changed to a plural one.)

A Shift in Person

It is important to avoid shifting unnecessarily among first person (*I, we*), second person (*you*), and third person (*she, he, it, one, they*). Such shifts can cause confusion:

INCORRECT	Most people (third person) who run for office find that if you (second person tell the truth during your campaign, you will gain the voters' respect.
CORRECT	Most people who run for office find that if they tell the truth during their campaigns, they will gain the voters' respect.
INCORRECT	One (first person) cannot tell whether they (third person) are suited for public office until they decide to run.
CORRECT	One cannot tell whether one is suited for public office until one decides to run.

2.10 Quotation Marks

It can be difficult to remember when to use quotation marks and where they go in relation to other punctuation. When faced with these questions, unpracticed writers often try to rely on logic rather than on a rule book, but the rules do not always seem to rely on logic. The only way to make sure of your use of quotation marks is to memorize the rules. Luckily, there are not many.

The Use of Quotation Marks

Use quotation marks to enclose direct quotations that are no longer than 100 words or eight typed lines:

> In his farewell address to the American people, George Washington warned, "The great rule of conduct for us, in regard to foreign nations, is, in extending our commercial relations, to have with them as little political connection as possible."

Longer quotations, called *block quotations*, are placed in a double-spaced indented block, without quotation marks:

> Lincoln clearly explained his motive for continuing the Civil War in his August 22, 1862, response to Horace Greeley's open letter:
>
>> I would save the Union. I would save it the shortest way under the Constitution. The sooner the National authority can be restored, the nearer the Union will be the Union as it was. If there be those who would not save the Union unless they could at the same time save Slavery, I do not agree with them. If there be those who would not save the Union unless they could at the same time destroy Slavery, I do not agree with them. (Lincoln 1946, 652)

Use single quotation marks to set off quotations within quotations:

> "I intend," said the senator, "to use in my speech a line from Frost's poem, 'The Road Not Taken.'"

■ **Note:** When the quote occurs at the end of the sentence, both the single and double quotation marks are placed outside the period.

Use quotation marks to set off titles of the following:

■ Short poems (those not printed as a separate volume)
■ Short stories
■ Articles or essays
■ Songs
■ Episodes of television or radio shows

Use quotation marks to set off words or phrases used in special ways:

■ To convey irony:

The "liberal" administration has done nothing but cater to big business.

■ To indicate a technical term:

To "filibuster" is to delay legislation, usually through prolonged speech-making. The last notable filibuster occurred just last week in the Senate. (Once the term is defined, it is not placed in quotation marks again.)

Quotation Marks in Relation to Other Punctuation

Place commas and periods *inside* closing quotation marks:

"My fellow Americans," said the president, "there are tough times ahead of us."

Place colons and semicolons *outside* closing quotation marks:

In his speech on voting, the governor warned against "an encroaching indolence"; he was referring to the middle class.

There are several victims of the government's campaign to "Turn Back the Clock": the homeless, the elderly, the mentally impaired.

Use the context to determine whether to place question marks, exclamation points, and dashes inside or outside closing quotation marks. If the punctuation is part of the quotation, place it inside the quotation mark:

"When will Congress make up its mind?" asked the ambassador.

The demonstrators shouted, "Free the hostages!" and "No more slavery!"

If the punctuation is not part of the quotation, place it outside the quotation mark:

Which president said, "We have nothing to fear but fear itself"?

■ **Note:** Although the quote is a complete sentence, you do not place a period after it. There can only be one piece of "terminal" punctuation (punctuation that ends a sentence).

2.11   Semicolons

The semicolon is a little-used punctuation mark that you should learn to incorporate into your writing strategy because of its many potential applications. For example, a semicolon can be used to correct a comma splice:

INCORRECT   The union representatives left the meeting in good spirits, their demands were met.

CORRECT   The union representatives left the meeting in good spirits; their demands were met.

INCORRECT   Several guests at the fundraiser had lost their invitations, however, we were able to seat them anyway.

CORRECT   Several guests at the fundraiser had lost their invitations; however, we were able to seat them anyway.

It is important to remember that conjunctive adverbs such as *however, therefore,* and *thus* are not coordinating words (such as *and, but, or, for, so, yet*) and cannot be used with a comma to link independent clauses. If the second independent clause begins with *however*, it must be preceded by either a period or a semicolon. As you can see from the second example above, connecting two independent clauses with a semicolon instead of a period preserves the suggestions that there is a strong relationship between the clauses.

Semicolons can also separate items in a series when the series items themselves contain commas:

The newspaper account of the rally stressed the march, which drew the biggest crowd; the mayor's speech, which drew tremendous applause; and the party in the park, which lasted for hours.

Avoid misusing semicolons. For example, use a comma, not a semicolon, to separate an independent clause from a dependent clause:

INCORRECT   Students from the college volunteered to answer phones during the pledge drive; which was set up to generate money for the new arts center.

CORRECT   Students from the college volunteered to answer phones during the pledge drive, which was set up to generate money for the new arts center.

Do not overuse semicolons. Although they are useful, too many semicolons in your writing can distract your readers' attention. Avoid monotony by using semicolons sparingly.

2.12   Sentence Fragments

A *fragment* is an incomplete part of a sentence that is punctuated and capitalized as if it were an entire sentence. It is an especially disruptive error because it obscures the connections that the words of a sentence must make in order to complete the reader's understanding.

Students sometimes write fragments because they are concerned that a sentence needs to be shortened. Remember that cutting the length of a sentence merely by adding a period somewhere often creates a fragment. When checking a writing for fragments, it is essential that you read each sentence carefully to determine whether it has (1) a complete subject and a verb; and (2) a subordinating word before the subject and verb, which makes the construction a subordinate clause rather than a complete sentence.

Some fragments lack a verb:

INCORRECT	The chairperson of our committee, receiving a letter from the mayor. (Watch out for words that look like verbs but are being used in another way.)
CORRECT	The chairperson of our committee received a letter from the mayor.

Some fragments lack a subject:

INCORRECT	Our study shows that there is broad support for improvement in the health-care system. And in the unemployment system.
CORRECT	Our study shows that there is broad support for improvement in the health care system and in the unemployment system.

Some fragments are subordinate clauses:

INCORRECT	After the latest edition of the newspaper came out. [This clause has the two major components of a complete sentence: a subject (*edition*) and a verb (*came*). Indeed, if the first word (*After*) were deleted, the clause would be a complete sentence. But that first word is a *subordinating word*, which prevents the following clause from standing on its own as a complete sentence. Watch out for this kind of construction. It is called a *subordinate clause*, and it is not a sentence.]
CORRECT	After the latest edition of the newspaper came out, the mayor's press secretary was overwhelmed with phone calls. (A common method of correcting a subordinate clause that has been punctuated as a complete sentence is to connect it to the complete sentence to which it is closest in meaning.)

INCORRECT   Several representatives asked for copies of the vice president's position paper. Which called for reform of the Environmental Protection Agency.

CORRECT   Several representatives asked for copies of the vice president's position paper, which called for reform of the Environmental Protection Agency.

2.13   Spelling

All of us have problems spelling certain words that we have not yet committed to memory. But most writers are not as bad at spelling as they believe they are. Usually an individual finds only a handful of words troubling. It is important to be as sensitive as possible to your own particular spelling problems—and to keep a dictionary handy. There is no excuse for failing to check spelling.

What follows is a list of commonly confused words and a list of commonly misspelled words. Read through the lists, looking for those words that tend to give you trouble. If you have any questions, consult your dictionary.

Commonly Confused Words

accept/except	desert/dessert	lessen/lesson
advice/advise	device/devise	loose/lose
affect/effect	die/dye	may be/maybe
aisle/isle	dominant/dominate	miner/minor
allusion/illusion	elicit/illicit	moral/morale
an/and	eminent/immanent/	of/off
angel/angle	imminent	passed/past
ascent/assent	envelop/envelope	patience/patients
bare/bear	every day/everyday	peace/piece
brake/break	fair/fare	personal/personnel
breath/breathe	formally/formerly	plain/plane
buy/by	forth/fourth	precede/proceed
capital/capitol	hear/here	presence/presents
choose/chose	heard/herd	principal/principle
cite/sight/site	hole/whole	quiet/quite
complement/compliment	human/humane	rain/reign/rein
conscience/conscious	its/it's	raise/raze
corps/corpse	know/no	reality/realty
council/counsel	later/latter	respectfully/respectively
dairy/diary	lay/lie	reverend/reverent
descent/dissent	lead/led	right/rite/write

road/rode

scene/seen

sense/since

stationary/stationery

straight/strait

taught/taut

than/then

their/there/they're

threw/through

too/to/two

track/tract

waist/waste

waive/wave

weak/week

weather/whether

were/where

which/witch

whose/who's

your/you're

Commonly Misspelled Words

acceptable

accessible

accommodate

accompany

accustomed

acquire

against

annihilate

apparent

arguing

argument

authentic

before

begin

beginning

believe

benefited

bulletin

business

cannot

category

committee

condemn

courteous

definitely

dependent

desperate

develop

different

disappear

disappoint

easily

efficient

environment

equipped

exceed

exercise

existence

experience

fascinate

finally

foresee

forty

fulfill

gauge

guaranteed

guard

harass

hero

heroes

humorous

hurried

hurriedly

hypocrite

ideally

immediately

immense

incredible

innocuous

intercede

interrupt

irrelevant

irresistible

irritate

knowledge

license

likelihood

maintenance

manageable

meanness

mischievous

missile

necessary

nevertheless

no one

noticeable

noticing

nuisance

occasion

occasionally

occurred

occurrences

omission

omit

opinion
opponent
parallel
parole
peaceable
performance
pertain
practical
preparation
probably
process
professor
prominent
pronunciation
psychology
publicly
pursue
pursuing
questionnaire
realize
receipt
received
recession
recommend

referring
religious
remembrance
reminisce
repetition
representative
rhythm
ridiculous
roommate
satellite
scarcity
scenery
science
secede
secession
secretary
senseless
separate
sergeant
shining
significant
sincerely
skiing
stubbornness

studying
succeed
success
successfully
susceptible
suspicious
technical
temporary
tendency
therefore
tragedy
truly
tyranny
unanimous
unconscious
undoubtedly
until
vacuum
valuable
various
vegetable
visible
without
women

CHAPTER 3

Generate an Effective Style

3.1 The Competent Writer

Good writing places your thoughts in your readers' minds in exactly the way you want them to be there. Good writing tells your readers just what you want them to know without telling them anything you do not want them to know. This may sound odd, but the fact is that writers have to be careful not to let unwanted messages slip into their writing. Look, for example, at the passage below, taken from a paper analyzing the impact of a worker-retraining program. Hidden within the prose is a message that jeopardizes the paper's success. Can you detect the message?

> Recent articles written on the subject of dislocated workers have had little to say about the particular problems dealt with in this paper. Because few of these articles focus on the problem at the state level.

Chances are, when you reached the end of the second "sentence," you detected a *sentence fragment* (explained in Chapter 2, section 2.12, page 46). *Sentence fragment* conveys to the reader a message that no writer wants to send: that the writer either is careless or, worse, has not mastered the language. Language errors such as fragments, misplaced commas, or shifts in verb tense send out warnings in readers' minds. As a result, readers lose some of their concentration on the issue being discussed; they become distracted and begin to wonder about the language competency of the writer. The writing loses effectiveness.

■ **Note:** Whatever goal you set for your paper—whether to persuade, describe, analyze, or speculate—you must also set one other goal: to display language competence. If your paper does not meet this goal, it will not completely achieve its other aims. Language errors spread doubt like a virus; they jeopardize all the hard work you have done on your paper.

Language competence is especially important in political science, for credibility in politics depends on such skill. Anyone who doubts this should remember the beating that Vice President Dan Quayle took in the press for misspelling the word *potato* at a 1992 spelling bee. His error caused a storm of humiliating publicity for the hapless Quayle, adding to an impression of his general incompetence.

Correctness is Relative

Although they may seem minor, the sort of language errors we are discussing—often called *surface errors*—can be extremely damaging in certain kinds of writing. Surface errors come in a variety of types, including misspellings, punctuation problems, grammar errors, and the inconsistent use of abbreviations, capitalization, and numerals. These errors are an affront to your readers' notion of correctness, and therein lies one of the biggest problems with surface errors. Different audiences tolerate different levels of correctness. You know that you can get away with surface errors in, say, a letter to a friend, who will probably not judge you harshly for them, whereas those same errors in a job application letter might eliminate you from consideration for the position. Correctness depends to an extent on context.

Another problem is that the rules governing correctness shift over time. What would have been an error to your grandmother's generation—the splitting of an infinitive, for example, or the ending of a sentence with a preposition—is taken in stride by most readers today.

So how do you write correctly when the rules shift from person to person and over time? Here are some tips:

Consider Your Audience

One of the great risks of writing is that even the simplest of choices regarding wording or punctuation can sometimes prejudice your audience against you in ways that may seem unfair. For example, look again at the old grammar rule forbidding the splitting of infinitives. After decades of telling students to never split an infinitive (something just done in this sentence), most composition experts now concede that a split infinitive is *not* a grammar crime. But suppose you have written a position paper trying to convince your city council of the need to hire security personnel for the library, and half of the council members—the people you wish to convince—remember their eighth-grade grammar teacher's warning about splitting infinitives. How will they respond when you tell them, in your introduction, that librarians are compelled "to always accompany" visitors to the rare book room because of the threat of vandalism? How much of their attention have you suddenly lost because of their automatic recollection of what is now a nonrule? It is possible, in other words, to write correctly and still offend your readers' notions of language competence.

Make sure that you tailor the surface features and the degree of formality of your writing to the level of competency that your readers require. When in doubt, take a conservative approach. Your audience might be just as distracted by a contraction as by a split infinitive.

Aim for Consistency

When dealing with a language question for which there are different answers—such as whether to use a comma before the conjunction in a series of three ("The mayor's speech addressed taxes, housing for the poor, and the job situation.")—always use

the same strategy throughout your paper. If, for example, you avoid splitting one infinitive, avoid splitting *all* infinitives.

Have Confidence in What You Know About Writing!

It is easy for unpracticed writers to allow their occasional mistakes to shake their
confidence in their writing ability. The fact is, however, that most of what we know
about writing is correct. We are all capable, for example, of writing grammatically
sound phrases, even if we cannot list the rules by which we achieve coherence. Most
writers who worry about their chronic errors make fewer mistakes than they think.
Becoming distressed about errors makes writing even more difficult.

3.2 Arguing Effectively

Although many papers written for political science classes strive to draw objective
conclusions from precise observations about politics and government, some assignments ask you to state, clarify, and defend your position on a current political issue.
When you do so, you create what philosophers call an *argument*. In common terms,
an argument is simply an oral disagreement about something. Some people like to
"argue" just to hear themselves talk (you may know someone like this). In this type
of argument all kinds of statements are tossed back and forth. Some may have merit,
but many are dubious, and some are downright silly. For philosophers and political
scientists, arguments are reasoned, logical attempts to persuade someone that something is true. In your political science paper, be sure to argue the way philosophers
do. Let's give it a try.

An argument as conducted within the discipline of political science contains three
specific properties: *conclusions, premises,* and *evidence*. A *conclusion* is the goal of
the argument, the point the argument is trying to make. *Premises* are statements made
to support a conclusion. For example, let's suppose that I say "Republicans are conservative, and conservatives oppose tax increases; therefore Republicans oppose tax
increases." In this statement, the phrases "Republicans are conservative," and "conservatives oppose tax increases" are both premises, and the phrase "Republicans
oppose tax increases" is my conclusion. Now, in most simple terms, the effectiveness
of my conclusion depends upon the strength of my premises. Therefore, we may be as-
sured that my conclusion "Republicans oppose tax increases" is only as convincing as
the premises ("Republicans are conservative," and "conservatives oppose tax increases") that I use to support it.

This is where *evidence* comes in. If I want people to believe my conclusion that
Republicans oppose tax increases, then I need to produce evidence to support my
premises that Republicans are conservative and conservatives oppose tax increases.
Evidence for this argument may include polls or interviews or statements about tax
increases by people who identify themselves as Republicans or conservatives.

Now here is where arguing gets technically tricky. A convincing argument
needs to be both *valid* and *cogent*. Oddly enough, an argument is considered technically *valid* if its conclusion can undoubtedly be drawn from its premises—*even*

if its premises are false. For example, the following argument, which may sound silly or hard to square with what we know of people in the real world, is nevertheless valid because its conclusion follows naturally from its admittedly far-fetched premises: "All Democrats eat pears. Meghan is a democrat. Meghan, therefore eats pears."

What about the following argument? "All Democrats eat pears. Meghan is a Republican. Meghan, therefore eats pears." Is it valid? No. The premises do not add up logically to the conclusion. So validity refers simply to the structural integrity of the argument, not to the question of whether the premises on which the argument is based happen to be true.

An argument is said to be *cogent* if (1) it is valid, and (2) its premises are true. The following argument is cogent. "All people born before 1850 are dead. Abraham Lincoln was born before 1850. Abraham Lincoln is dead."

To make convincing arguments, then, you need cogent reasoning: valid arguments and true premises based upon sound evidence. How do you know if the evidence is sound? The best test is to examine the methods by which the evidence was produced. Strong scholarship uses rigorous, verifiable methods and is therefore an unusually reliable source of information. Less reliable is information from sources that have strong ideological biases, because such sources often reflect those biases.

3.3 Forms of Argument

To help us determine the extent to which particular arguments are cogent, philosophers have classified them into a variety of forms. Understanding these forms will help you precisely identify errors in your own arguments and those of others.

- *Modus ponens* is a good place to begin. A modus ponens is a valid argument that identifies a certain chain of relationships. "If I invent a safe, effective pill to make short people tall, I will become rich. I have invented a safe, effective pill to make short people tall, and so I am rich." "If I drink too much I can drive home or let my girlfriend drive. I drank too much. Therefore I can drive or just ride."
- A *modus tollens* is similar but identifies an inverse chain of relationships. "If President Obama appoints three justices to the Supreme Court, the Court will be more liberal. The Court will not become more liberal, therefore President Obama will not appoint three justices to the Supreme Court."
- A **tautology** is an argument that is always, universally, true because it cannot be false. "A senator is not a carrot; clear diamonds are clear; a good rat is a rat."
- A **contradiction** is a statement that is always false. "I am voting tomorrow and I am not voting tomorrow." "I own a cat and I don't own a cat."
- A **syllogism** makes what sounds like a logical connection among sets of phenomena. The problem with many syllogisms is that words often have multiple meanings. "God is love. Love is blind. Stevie Wonder is blind. Stevie Wonder is

God." Syllogisms may also be true. "All humans die. Grady is a human. Grady will die." But whether true or false, most syllogisms do not tell you much.

- A **dilemma** sets up a situation with choices, but only undesirable consequences from them. "I will eat a lot or I will go on a diet. If I eat a lot I will get fat. If I go on a diet I will be hungry. Therefore, I will either get fat or go hungry."
- **Reductio ad absurdum** sets up a chain of possibilities even more ridiculous than many dilemmas. "Suppose I climb Mount Everest. If I climb Mount Everest I will cancel my subscription to *Industrial Waste Management*. If I cancel my subscription to *Industrial Waste Management*, then my sister will buy a dairy farm. My sister will not buy a dairy farm. Therefore, I will not climb Mount Everest."
- An **analogy** draws a conclusion based upon widely observed patterns. "Most middle school students wear tee shirts, play soccer, eat hamburgers, and ride bicycles. My grandfather wears tee shirts, plays soccer, eats hamburgers, and rides a bicycle. Therefore my grandfather is a middle school student."
- A popular form of argument is **induction by elimination**. In this process you identify all the probable solutions to a problem or question, then eliminate those that don't work until you are left with one. The one that remains is therefore the correct one.
- A **statistical induction** relies on probability. "The sun has come up every morning for a billion years; therefore it will rise tomorrow."
- An **inference to best explanation** finds a cause in a likely place. "Whenever I pick berries with Uncle Fred I feel fine, but when I pick berries with Aunt Agnes I break out in hives. Therefore, Aunt Agnes gives me hives."

Can you determine which of these forms of argument is being used in the following paragraph? Is the argument valid? Is it cogent?

3.4   Fallacies

Fallacies are invalid forms of argument. They may be *formal*, meaning they have an invalid structure, or *informal*, meaning their content is false or inadequate. We shall examine some common formal fallacies first.

- When we **assume the antecedent**, we fail to carefully identify all relevant possibilities.

    If Sarah Palin becomes president, I can retire. Sarah Palin cannot become president, therefore I cannot retire.

The problem with this argument is that I may be able to retire whether or not Sarah Palin becomes president.

- When **we reverse the consequent**, we may come to the wrong conclusion.

    When I get old, I will die.

This statement ignores the fact that I could die at a young age.

■ An **exclusive fallacy** occurs when two possibilities presented as mutually exclusive are not genuinely mutually exclusive.

> I will either take the train or a bus to work tomorrow. Since I will not take a train or a bus, I will not go to work tomorrow.

In fact, I could take both a train and a bus, or neither, to go to work tomorrow.

Now we turn to *informal* fallacies.

■ **Invalid correlations** occur when coincidences become causes. Just because most senators are millionaires, being a millionaire may not get you a senate seat.

■ **Invalid appeals** to authority occur often in advertising. The fact that Tiger Woods is an excellent golfer does not mean we should buy a Buick.

■ A **straw person** misrepresents an opinion by substituting a distorted and unattractive view of it. When Rush Limbaugh calls feminists "Feminazis," he is comparing one group of people with another that is held in contempt.

■ **Inconsistency** occurs when conflicting premises are used to support a conclusion. If you claim that pitbulls are friendly dogs but admit that they cause more injuries than any other breed, you are being inconsistent.

■ When you fail to consider all available alternatives, you may produce a **false dilemma**. If you say "I must have this operation now or never," you have probably ignored some other choices.

■ A **complex question** is an attempt to get someone to agree to something while answering a different question. "When are the Republicans going to cut spending?" is a question intended to get you to admit Republicans have not cut spending.

■ **Begging the question** embeds in the premises of the argument the notion that the conclusion is true. "God exists because it says so in the Bible, which is a trustworthy source because it was written by God."

■ **Suppressing evidence** is a common fallacy that occurs in many forms. "Democrats are always the ones to increase the national debt."

■ In **lack of proportion**, the value of something is underestimated or exaggerated. "This Hummer is just what you need to take the kids to soccer practice."

■ **Appeals to unknowable statistics** are also popular. "The French are always willing to take advantage of someone."

■ *Ad hominem* is an attack on an irrelevant aspect of a person. "Jason is unreliable. He spends all his time reading."

■ **Guilt by association** is similar to the *ad hominem* fallacy. "Jason is unreliable. He spends all his time with Tony."

■ **Two wrongs make a right** is an attempt to support a bad decision based upon another bad decision. "The Democrats increased the deficit, so we might as well, too."

■ **Equivocation** uses two meanings of the same word in inappropriate contexts. "Freedom is what it's all about, and we need to be free from Muslims."

■ An **appeal to ignorance** is made when we persuade someone that her failure to prove her argument means that it is false.

- We commit **composition** when we attribute to a whole group the characteristics of one or some of its members. The fact that some AlQaeda operatives are Saudis does not mean that all Saudis support AlQaeda.
- **Division** is an inverse of composition. To say that "Oregon Pinot Noir is the best wine in the country" does not mean that every bottle of Oregon pinot noir will be as good as the rest.
- We draw a **hasty conclusion** when, upon finding wonderful lasagna at an Italian restaurant, we assume that all Italian restaurants serve wonderful lasagna.
- A **questionable cause** occurs when insufficient evidence is accepted for a particular phenomenon. A particular campaign commercial, for example, may or may not lead to a candidate's defeat.
- **Questionable analogies** occur when we overlook obvious differences between things. "I know that Candidate Leghorn will make a great president because he was a great governor."
- Sometimes we **appeal to pity** when our argument is weak. "I know I didn't study for the test, but if I fail, I'll lose my scholarship."
- Other times we **appeal to the stick**. "If you lose your scholarship you will not go to Cancun on spring break."
- In yet other situations we **appeal to loyalty**. "Your father may have left you at that gas station in Muskogee, but he is still your father."
- An **appeal to popularity** often demonstrates a lack of sound judgment. "But Mom, everybody drag races to the edge of the canyon."
- We practice **provincialism** when we maintain that our way of doing things is better than the way others do them. "American democracy is the only way to govern."
- We support a **double standard** when some people can do things others can't. It seems to be easier to forgive members of the parish for being unfaithful than it is to forgive the pastor.
- Finally, some people are adept at **invincible ignorance**. They are proud of refusing to listen to anything from someone with whom they disagree. Invincible ignorance is prevalent in times of war and political polarization.

It is vital for the political scientist to be able to identify fallacies precisely in his or her own arguments and in the arguments of others. Sound arguments not only persuade and educate people; they are essential to formulating the sort of decisions that make government effective and democracy viable.

CHAPTER 4
Format Your Paper Correctly

Scholarship, or scholarly writing, is composed of carefully drawn conclusions based upon meticulous observations and precise measurements. One of its great goals is credibility, and the more credible it is, the likelier it is to withstand challenges than are writings based solely upon instinct, insight, or opinion. Producing good quality scholarship, therefore, provides you with substantial credibility among many groups of people, especially those in authority.

But there is a price to be paid for this credibility. Accepted scholarship follows a good many rules. A significant part of what you learn in college is how to master these rules. The four categories of rules most important to good scholarship are (1) formats, (2) data presentation, (3) source citation, and (4) originality (producing your own original work and avoiding plagiarism). In this chapter we will cover format and presentation and in Chapter 5, citation and avoiding plagiarism will be detailed.

Your format makes your paper's first impression. Justly or not, accurately or not, it announces your professional competence—or lack of competence. A well-executed format implies that your paper is worth reading. More importantly, however, a proper format brings information to your readers in a familiar form that has the effect of setting their minds at ease. Your paper's format should therefore impress your readers with your academic competence as a political scientist by following accepted professional standards. Like the style and clarity of your writing, your format communicates messages that are often more readily and profoundly received than the content of the document itself.

The formats described in this chapter are in conformance with generally accepted standards in the discipline of political science, including instructions for the following elements:

General page formats	Table of contents
Title page	Reference page
Abstract	List of tables and figures
Executive summary	Text
Outline page	Appendixes

■ **Note:** Except for special instructions from your instructor, follow the directions in this manual exactly.

4.1   General Page Formats

Political science assignments should be printed on 8-by-11-inch premium white bond paper, 20 pound or heavier. Do not use any other size or color except to comply with special instructions from your instructor, and do not use off-white or poor quality (draft) paper. Political science that is worth the time to write and read is worth good paper.

Always submit to your instructor an original typed or computer-printed manuscript. Do not submit a photocopy! Always make a second paper copy and back up your electronic copy for your own files in case the original is lost.

Margins, except in theses and dissertations, should be one inch on all sides of the paper. Unless otherwise instructed, all papers should be double-spaced in a 12-point word-processing font or typewriter pica type. Typewriter elite type may be used if another is not available. Select a font that is plain and easy to read, such as Helvetica, Courier, Garamond, or Times Roman. Do not use script, stylized, or elaborate fonts.

Page numbers should appear in the upper right-hand corner of each page, starting immediately after the title page. No page number should appear on the title page or on the first page of the text. Page numbers should appear one inch from the right side and one-half inch from the top of the page. They should proceed consecutively beginning with the title page (although the first number is not actually printed on the title page). You may use lowercase roman numerals (i, ii, iii, iv, v, vi, vii, viii, ix, x, and so on) for the pages, such as the title page, table of contents, and table of figures, that precede the first page of text, but if you use them, the numbers must be placed at the center of the bottom of the page.

Ask your instructor about bindings. In the absence of further directions, do not bind your paper or enclose it within a plastic cover sheet. Place one staple in the upper left-hand corner, or use a paper clip at the top of the paper. Note that a paper to be submitted to a journal for publication should not be clipped, stapled, or bound in any form.

4.2   Title Page

The following information will be centered on the title page:

Title of the paper

Name of writer

Course name, section number, and instructor

College or university

Date

The Second Bush Presidency

by

Nicole Ashley Linscheid

The American Presidency

POL213

Dr. Zaphod Brown

St. Johns University

January 1, 2010

As the sample title page above shows, the title should clearly describe the problem addressed in the paper. If the paper discusses juvenile recidivism in Albemarle County jails, for example, the title "Recidivism in the Albemarle County Criminal Justice System" is professional, clear, and helpful to the reader. "Albemarle County," "Juvenile Justice," or "County Jails" are all too vague to be effective. Also, the title should not be "cute." A cute title may attract attention for a play on Broadway, but it will detract from the credibility of a paper in political science. "Inadequate Solid Waste Disposal Facilities in Denver" is professional. "Down in the Dumps" is not.

In addition, title pages for position papers and policy analysis papers must include the name, title, and organization of the public official who has the authority and responsibility to implement the recommendation of your paper. The person to whom you address the paper should be the person who has the responsibility and the authority to make the decision that is called for in your paper. The "address" should include the person's name, title, and organization, as shown in the example of a title page for a position paper that follows. To identify the appropriate official, first carefully define the problem and the best solution. Then ascertain the person or persons who have the authority to solve the problem. If you recommend installation of a traffic signal at a particular intersection, for example, find out who makes the decisions regarding such actions in your community. It may be the public safety director, a transportation planning commission, or a town council.

Oak City Police Department Personnel Policy Revisions

submitted to

Farley Z. Simmons

Director of Personnel

Police Department

Oak City, Arkansas

by

Luke Tyler Linscheid

American National Government

GOV 1001

Dr. James Stonecipher

Randolph Scott College

January 21, 2006

4.3   Abstract

An abstract is a brief summary of a paper written primarily to allow potential readers to see if the paper contains information of sufficient interest for them to read. People conducting research want specific kinds of information, and they often read dozens of abstracts looking for papers that contain relevant data. Abstracts have the designation "Abstract" centered near the top of the page. Next is the title, also centered, followed by a paragraph that precisely states the paper's topic, research and analysis methods, and results and conclusions. The abstract should be written in one paragraph of no more than 150 words. Remember, an abstract is not an introduction; instead, it is a summary, as demonstrated in the sample below.

Abstract

Bertrand Russell's View of Mysticism

This paper reviews Bertrand Russell's writings on religion, mysticism, and science, and defines his perspective of the contribution of mysticism to scientific knowledge. Russell drew a sharp distinction between what he considered to be (1) the essence of religion, and (2) dogma or assertions attached to religion by theologians and religious leaders. Although some of his writings, including *Why I Am Not a Christian*, appear hostile to all aspects of religion, Russell actually asserts that religion, freed from doctrinal encumbrances, not only fulfills certain psychological needs but evokes many of the most beneficial human impulses. He believes that religious mysticism generates an intellectual disinterestedness that may be useful to science, but that it is not a source of a special type of knowledge beyond investigation by science.

4.4   Executive Summary

An executive summary, like an abstract, summarizes the content of a paper but does so in more detail. A sample executive summary is given on next page. Whereas abstracts are read by people who are doing research, executive summaries are more likely to be read by people who need some or all of the information in the paper in order to make a decision. Many people, however, will read the executive summary to fix clearly in their mind the organization and results of a paper before reading the paper itself.

Executive Summary

Municipal parks in Springfield are deteriorating because of inadequate mainte-nance, and one park in particular, Oak Ridge Community Park, needs immediate attention. The problem is that parking, picnic, and restroom facilities at Oak Ridge Community Park have deteriorated as a result of normal wear, adverse weather, and vandalism, and are inadequate to meet public demand. The park was established as a public recreation "Class B" facility in 1967. Only one major ren-ovation has occurred: in the summer of 1987 general building repair was done, and new swing sets were installed. The Park Department estimates that 10,000 square feet of new parking space, fourteen items of playground equipment, seven-teen new picnic tables, and repairs on current facilities would cost about $43,700.

Three possible solutions have been given extensive consideration in this paper. One option is to do nothing. Area residents will use the area less as deterioration con-tinues, but no immediate outlay of public funds will be necessary. The first alternative solution is to make all repairs immediately. Area residents will enjoy immediate and increased use of facilities. Taxpayers have turned down the last three tax increase re-quests. Revenue bonds may be acceptable to a total of $20,000, according to the City Manager, but no more than $5,000 per year is available from general city revenues.

A second alternative is to make repairs, according to a priority list, over a five-year period, using a combination of general city revenues and a $20,000 first-year bond issue that will require City Council and voter approval. Residents will enjoy the most needed improvements immediately.

The recommendation of this report is that the second alternative be adopted by the City Council. The City Council should, during its May 15 meeting, (1) adopt a resolution of intent to commit $5,000 per year for five years from the general revenue fund, dedicated to this purpose; and (2) approve for submission to public vote in the November 2007 election a $20,000 bond issue.

4.5   Outline Page

An outline page is a specific type of executive summary. Most often found in position papers and policy analysis papers, an outline page provides more information about the organization of the paper than does an executive summary. The outline shows clearly the sections in the paper and the information in each. An outline page is an asset because it allows busy decision-makers to understand the entire content of a pa-per without reading it all or to refer quickly to a specific part for more information.

Position papers and policy analysis papers are written for people in positions of authority who normally need to make a variety of decisions in a short period. Outline pages reduce the amount of time these people need to understand a policy problem, the alternative solutions, and the author's preferred solution.

Outline pages sequentially list the complete topic sentences of the major paragraphs of a paper, in outline form. In a position paper, for example, you will be stating a problem, defining possible solutions, and then recommending the best solution. These three steps will be the major headings in your outline. (See Chapter 1 for instructions on writing an outline.) Wait until you have completed the paper before writing the outline page. Take the topic sentences from the leading (most important) paragraph in each section of your paper and place them in the appropriate places in your outline. A sample outline page is given on pages 63–64.

4.6   Table of Contents

A table of contents does not provide as much information as an outline, but it does include the titles of the major divisions and subdivisions of a paper. Tables of contents are not normally required in student papers or papers presented at professional meetings but may be included. They are normally required, however, in books, theses, and dissertations. The table of contents should consist of the chapter or main section titles, and the headings used in the text, with one additional level of titles, along with their page numbers, as the sample on page 84 demonstrates.

4.7   The Body of Your Paper

Text

Ask your instructor for the number of pages required for the paper you are writing. The text should follow the directions explained in Chapter 1 of this manual and should conform to the format shown below.

Sample Passage of Text

The problem is that parking, picnic, and restroom facilities at Oak Ridge Community Park have deteriorated as a result of normal wear, adverse weather, and vandalism, and are of inadequate quantity to meet public demand. The paved parking lot has crumbled and eroded. As many as two hundred cars park on the lawn during major holidays. Only one of the five swing sets is in safe operating condition. Each set accommodates four children, but during weekends and holidays many children wait turns for the available sets. Spray paint vandalism has marred the rest room facilities, which are inadequate to meet major holiday demands.

The Department of Parks and Recreation established the park as a public recreation Class B facility in 1963. In the summer of 1987, the department conducted general building repair and installed new steel swing sets. Only minimal annual maintenance has occurred since that time.

(Continued)

Sample Passage of Text *(Continued)*

The department estimates that 10,000 square feet of new parking lot space, fourteen items of playground equipment, seventeen new picnic tables, and repairs on current facilities would cost about $43,700 (Department of Parks and Recreation 2005). Parking lot improvements include a new surface of coarse gravel on the old paved lot and expansion of the new paved lot by 10,000 square feet. The State Engineering Office estimates the cost of parking lot improvements to be $16,200.

Chapter Headings

Your paper should include no more than three levels of headings:

1. *Primary*, which should be centered, in boldface, and using headline-style capitalization (each word except articles, prepositions, and conjunctions capitalized)
2. *Secondary*, which begins at the left margin, in boldface and also in headline style capitalization
3. *Tertiary*, which also begins at the left margin and uses headline style capitalization but is underlined instead of boldfaced and followed immediately by a period and the first line of the succeeding text.

The following illustration shows the proper use of chapter headings:

The House of Representatives	(Primary Heading)
Impeachment Procedures of the House	(Secondary Heading)
<u>Rules for Debate.</u> The first rule states that Congress . . .	(Tertiary Heading)

Reference Page

The format for references is discussed in detail in the source citation information that is contained in Chapter 5 of this manual.

4.8   Tables, Illustrations, Figures, and Appendixes

If your paper includes tables, illustrations, or figures, include a page after the Table of Contents listing each of them, under the name for it used in the paper's text. List the items in the order in which they appear in the paper, along with their page numbers. You may list tables, illustrations, and figures together under the title "Figures" (and call them all "Figures" in the text), or if you have more than a half page of entries, you may have separate lists for tables, illustrations, and figures (and title them accordingly in the text). An example of the format for such lists is given on page 65.

Outline of Contents

I. The problem is that parking, picnic, and restroom facilities at Oak Ridge Community Park have deteriorated as a result of normal wear, adverse weather, and vandalism, and are inadequate to meet public demand.

    A. Only one major renovation has occurred since 1967, when the park was opened.

    B. The Park Department estimates that 10,000 square feet of new parking space, fourteen items of playground equipment, seventeen new picnic tables, and repairs on current facilities would cost about $43,700.

II. The municipal government has given extensive consideration to three possible solutions.

    A. One option is to do nothing. Area residents will use the area less as deterioration continues, but no immediate outlay of public funds will be necessary.

    B. The first alternative solution is to make all repairs immediately. Area residents will enjoy immediate and increased use of facilities. $43,700 in funds will be needed. Sources include: (1) Community Development Block Grant funds; (2) increased property taxes; (3) revenue bonds; and (4) general city revenues.

    C. A second alternative is to make repairs according to a priority list over a five-year period, using a combination of general city revenues and a $20,000 first-year bond issue. Residents will enjoy the most needed improvements immediately. The bond issue will require City Council and voter approval.

III. The recommendation of this report is that alternative C be adopted by the City Council. The benefit/cost analysis demonstrates that residents will be satisfied if basic improvements are made immediately. The City Council should, during its May 15 meeting, (1) adopt a resolution of intent to commit $5,000 per year for five years from the general revenue fund, dedicated to this purpose; and (2) approve for submission to public vote in the November 2011 election a $20,000 bond issue.

Contents

Figures

Tables

Tables are used in the text to show relationships among data, to help the reader come to a conclusion or understand a certain point. Tables that show simple results or "raw" data should be placed in an appendix. Tables should not reiterate the content of the text. They should say something new, and they should stand on their own. In other words, the reader should be able to understand the table without reading the text. Clearly label the columns and rows in the table. Each word in the title (except articles, prepositions, and conjunctions) should be capitalized. The source of the information should be shown immediately below the table, not in a footnote or endnote. A sample table is shown below.

TABLE 1 Projections of the Total Population of Selected States, 2005–2035 (in thousands)					
State	**2005**	**2015**	**2025**	**2030**	**2035**
Alabama	4,253	4,451	4,631	4,956	5,224
Illinois	11,830	12,051	12,266	12,808	13,440
Maine	1,241	1,259	1,285	1,362	1,423
New Mexico	1,685	1,860	2,016	2,300	2,612
Oklahoma	3,278	3,373	3,491	3,789	4,057
Tennessee	5,256	5,657	5,966	6,365	6,665
Virginia	6,618	6,997	7,324	7,921	8,466

Source: U.S. Census Bureau.

Illustrations and Figures

Illustrations are not normally inserted in the text of a political science paper, even in an appendix, unless they are necessary to explain the content. If illustrations are necessary, do not paste or tape photocopies of photographs or similar materials to the text or the appendix. Instead, photocopy each one on a separate sheet of paper and center it, along with its typed title, within the normal margins of the paper. The format of illustration titles should be the same as that for tables and figures.

Figures in the form of charts and graphs may be very helpful in presenting certain types of information, as the example shows on page 65.

Appendixes

Appendixes are reference materials provided for the convenience of the reader at the back of the paper, after the text. Providing information that supplements the important facts in the text, they may include maps, charts, tables, and selected documents. Do not place materials that are merely interesting or decorative in your appendix. Use only items that will answer questions raised by the text or are necessary to explain the text. Follow the guidelines for formats for tables, illustrations, and figures when adding material in an appendix. At the top center of the page, label your first appendix "Appendix A," your second appendix "Appendix B," and so on. Do not append an entire government report, journal article, or other publication, but only the portions of such documents that are necessary to support your paper. The source of the information should always be evident on the appended pages.

CHAPTER 5

Cite Sources and Avoid Plagiarism

One of your most important jobs as a research writer is to document your use of source material carefully and clearly. Failure to do so will cause your reader confusion, damage the effectiveness of your paper, and perhaps make you vulnerable to a charge of plagiarism. Proper documentation is more than just good form. It is a powerful indicator of your own commitment to scholarship and the sense of authority that you bring to your writing. Good documentation demonstrates your expertise as a researcher and increases your reader's trust in you and your work.

Unfortunately, as anybody who has ever written a research paper knows, getting the documentation right can be a frustrating, confusing job, especially for the writer who is not familiar with the documentation system he or she is trying to use. Positioning each element of a single reference citation accurately can require a lot of time looking through the style manual. Even before you begin to work on the specific citations for your paper, there are important questions of style and format to answer.

5.1   What to Document

You must always credit direct quotes, as well as certain kinds of paraphrased material. Information that is basic—important dates, universally acknowledged facts, or commonly held opinions—need not be cited. Information that is not widely known, however, should receive documentation. This type of material includes ideas, evaluations, critiques, and descriptions original to your source.

What if you are unsure whether a certain fact is an academic "given" or sufficiently unique to warrant a citation? You are, after all, probably a newcomer to the field in which you are conducting your research. If in doubt, supply the documentation. It is better to overdocument than to fail to do justice to a source.

5.2   The Choice of Style

There are several documentation styles available, each designed to meet the needs of researchers in particular fields. The reference systems approved by the Modern Language Association (MLA) and the American Psychological Association (APA) are often used in the humanities and the social sciences and could serve the needs of the political science writer, but this manual offers the style most likely to be appropriate for political science papers: the APSA Author-Date System.

The American Political Science Association (APSA) has adopted a modification of the style elaborated in the *Chicago Manual of Style* (*CMS*), perhaps the most universally approved of all documentation authorities. One of the advantages of using the APSA style, which is outlined in an APSA pamphlet entitled *Style Manual for Political Science* (1993, revised August 2006), is that it is designed to guide the professional political scientist in preparing a manuscript for submission to the *American Political Science Review*, the journal of the American Political Science Association and the most influential political science journal in publication. Learning the APSA documentation style, then, offers you as a student another crucial connection to the world of the political scientist. For this reason, there are models below of formats described in the APSA *Style Manual* in addition to other models found only in the *CMS*.

■ **Note:** The APSA *Style Manual* for Political Science covers only certain basic reference and bibliographical models. For other models and for more detailed suggestions about referencing format, the 2006 revised edition of the APSA *Style Manual* refers readers to the "latest edition" of the *CMS*, which at the time was the fifteenth edition, published in 2003. The formats below are based on APSA guidelines, whenever such guidelines are available. Otherwise, the formats follow models taken from the fifteenth (2003) edition of the *CMS*, and, when necessary, from the more exhaustive fourteenth (1993) edition. Models based on the *CMS* are identified as such, with section numbers for relevant passages in the *CMS* given in parentheses, preceded by the number of the edition. For example, *CMS* 14 (15.367) refers to the 367th section of Chapter 15 in the fourteenth edition of the *Chicago Manual of Style*, a section that shows how to cite source material taken from the U.S. Constitution.

The Importance of Consistency

The most important rule regarding documentation of your work is to *be consistent*. Sloppy referencing undermines your reader's trust and does a disservice to the writers whose work you are incorporating into your own argument. From a purely practical standpoint, inconsistent referencing can severely damage your grade.

Using the Style Manual

Read through the guidelines in the following pages before trying to use them to structure your notes. Unpracticed student researchers tend to ignore this section of the style manual until the moment the first note has to be worked out, and then they skim through the examples looking for the one that perfectly corresponds to the immediate case in hand. But most style manuals do not include every possible documentation model, so the writer must piece together a coherent reference out of elements from several examples. Reading through all the examples before using them can give you a feel for the placement of information in citations for different kinds of sources—such as magazine articles, book chapters, government documents, and electronic texts—as well as for how the referencing system works in general.

When you use the author-date system of citation, you place a note, in parentheses, within the text, following the passage where your source material appears. In order not to distract the reader from the argument, make the reference as brief as possible, containing just enough information to refer the reader to the full citation in the reference list following the text. Usually the minimum information necessary is the author's last name, the date of the publication of the source, and if you are referring to a specific passage instead of the entire work, the page number(s) of the passage you are using. As indicated by the models below, this information can be given in a number of ways.

Models of full citations that correspond to these parenthetical text references are given in the subsection that begins on page 75. A sample reference list appears on pages 82–83.

5.3 The Author-Date System: Citations

Author, Date, and Page in Parentheses

Several critics found the senator's remarks to be, in the words of one, "hopelessly off the mark and dangerously incendiary" (Northrup 2006, 28).

Note that, when it appears at the end of a sentence, the parenthetical reference is placed inside the period.

Page and Chapter in Notes

A text citation may refer to an entire article, in which case you need not include page numbers, since they are given in the reference list at the end of the paper. However, you will sometimes need to cite specific page and chapter numbers, which follow the date and are preceded by a comma and, in the case of a chapter, the abbreviation *chap*. Note that you do not use the abbreviation *p.* or *pp.* when referring to page numbers.

Page Numbers.

Randalson (2004, 84–86) provides a brief but coherent description of the bill's evolution.

Chapter Numbers.

Collins (2006, chaps. 9, 10) discusses at length the structure of the Roman senate.

Author and Date in Text.   The following example focuses the reader's attention on Northrup's article:

For a highly critical review of the senator's performance, see Northrup 2006 (28).

Author in the Text, Date and Page in Parentheses.   Here the emphasis is on the author, for only Northrup's name appears within the grammar of the sentence:

> Northrup (2006, 28) called the senator's remarks "hopelessly off the mark and dangerously incendiary."

Source with Two Authors.

> The administration's efforts at reforming the education system are drawing more praise than condemnation (Younger and Petty 2005).

Notice that the names are not necessarily arranged alphabetically. Use the order that the authors themselves sanctioned on the title page of the book or article.

Source with Three Authors.

> Most of the farmers in the region support the cooperative's new pricing plan (Moore, Macrory, and Traylor 2004, 132).

Source with Four or More Authors.   Place the Latin phrase *et al.*, meaning "and others," after the name of the first author. Note that the phrase appears in roman type, not italics, and is followed by a period:

> According to Herring et al. (2004, 42), five builders backed out of the project due to doubts about the local economy.

More Than One Source.   Note that the references are arranged alphabetically:

> Several commentators have supported the council's decision to expand the ruling (Barrere 2004; Grady 2004; Payne 2004).

Two Authors with the Same Last Name.   Use a first initial to differentiate two authors with the same last name:

> Research suggests that few taxpayers will appreciate the new budget cuts (B. Grady 2005; L. Grady 2004).

Two Works by the Same Author.   If two references by the same author appear in the same note, place a comma between the publication dates:

> George (2010, 2007) argues for sweeping tax reform on the national level.

If the two works were published in the same year, differentiate them by adding lowercase letters to the publication dates. Be sure to add the letters to the reference list, too:

> The commission's last five annual reports pointed out the same weaknesses in the structure of the city government (Estrada 2009a, 2009b).

Reprints. It is sometimes significant to note the date when an important text was first published, even if you are using a reprint of that work. In this case, the date of the first printing appears in brackets before the date of the reprint:

> During that period, there were three advertising campaign strategies that were deemed potentially useful to political campaigners (Adams [1990] 2010, 12).

Classic Texts. You may use the author-date system to structure notes for classic texts, such as the Bible, standard translations of ancient Greek works, or numbers of *The Federalist Papers*, by citing the date and page numbers of the edition you are using. Or you may refer to these texts by using the systems by which they are subdivided. Since all editions of a classic text employ the same standard subdivisions, this reference method has the advantage of allowing your reader to find the citation in any published version of the text. For example, you may cite a biblical passage by referring to the particular book, chapter, and verse, all in roman type, with the translation given after the verse number. Titles of books of the Bible should be abbreviated:

> "But the path of the just is as the shining light, that shineth more and more unto the perfect day" (Prov. 4:18 King James Version).

The Federalist Papers may be cited by their standard numbers:

> Madison addresses the problem of factions in a republic (*Federalist* 10).

Public Documents. According to the 2006 revised edition of the APSA *Style Manual*, you may cite public documents using the standard author-date technique. The *Style Manual* recommends consulting the fifteenth edition of *CMS* (17.290–356) and Chapter 12 of the latest edition of Kate L. Turabian's *Manual for Writers of Term Papers, Theses, and Dissertations* (Univ. of Chicago Press, 2004) for more detailed information. While the 2006 APSA *Style Manual* provides models of reference list entries for a few types of government documents, neither it nor the fifteenth edition of *CMS* (2003) offers corresponding examples of parenthetical text citations. The following models are based, therefore, on information taken from the APSA *Style Manual* and from Chapters 15 and 16 of the fourteenth edition of *CMS* (1993).

Congressional Journals. Parenthetical text references to either the *Senate Journal* or the *House Journal* start with the journal title in place of the author, the session year, and, if applicable, the page:

> Senator Jones endorsed the proposal as reworded by Senator Edward's committee (*U.S. Senate Journal* 2006, 24).

Congressional Debates. Congressional debates are printed in the daily issues of the *Congressional Record*, which are bound biweekly and then collected and bound at the end of the session. Whenever possible, you should consult the bound yearly collection instead of the biweekly compilations. Your parenthetical reference should begin with the title *Congressional Record* (or *Cong. Rec.*) in place of the author's

name and include the year of the congressional session, the volume and part of the
Congressional Record, and finally the page:

> Rep. Valentine and Rep. Beechnut addressed the question of funding for
> secondary education (*Cong. Rec.* 1930, 72, pt. 8: 9012).

Congressional Reports and Documents.   References to these reports and documents, which are numbered sequentially in one- or two-year periods, include the
name of the body generating the material, the year, and the page:

> Rep. Slavin promised from the floor to answer the charges against him within the
> next week (U.S. Congress. House 2006, 12–13).

■ **Note: You may omit the *U.S.*, if it is clear from the context that you are
referring to the United States. Whichever form you use, be sure to use
it consistently, in both the notes and the reference list.**

Bills and Resolutions.   Bills and resolutions from either house of Congress are
usually cited by title within the text, where the date and resolution number are also
sometimes given. Be sure to italicize the title:

> The *Visa Formalization Act of 2005* prohibits consular officials from rejecting visa
> requests out of hand (U.S. Congress. Senate 2005).

Statutes

Citing to the Statutes at Large. Bills or resolutions that have become law in a particular year are published in the annual volume of the *United States Statutes at Large* (in
legal abbreviation, *Stat.*) before being added to the *United States Code*. According to
CMS 15 (17.310), you may cite laws to either the *Statutes* or the *U.S. Code* or both:

> But FEMA's authority for carrying out the national flood insurance program was
> increased the next month (*National Flood Insurance Program Enhanced Borrow-
> ing Authority Act of* 2006, 317).

Citing to the U.S. Code. According to *CMS* 14 (16.165), once the law has been
incorporated into the *U.S. Code* it should be cited, by title, within the running text:

> But the next month FEMA's authority for carrying out the national flood
> insurance program was increased by the *National Flood Insurance Program
> Enhanced Borrowing Authority Act of 2006.*

United States Constitution.   According to *CMS* 14 (15.367), references to the
U.S. Constitution include the number of the article or amendment, the section number, and the clause, if necessary:

> The president has the power, in extraordinary circumstances, either to convene
> or to dismiss Congress (U.S. Constitution, art. 3, sec. 3).

■ **Note:** It is not necessary to include the Constitution in the reference list.

Executive Department Documents. A reference to a report, bulletin, circular, or any other type of material issued by the executive department starts with the name of the agency issuing the document, although you may use the name of the author, if known:

> Recent demographic projections suggest that city growth will continue to be lateral for several more years, as businesses flee downtown areas for the suburbs (Department of Labor 2004, 334).

Legal References

Supreme Court. As with laws, court decisions are rarely given their own parenthetical text citation and reference list entry, but are instead identified in the text. If you wish to use a formal reference, however, you may place within the parentheses the title of the case, in italics, followed by the source (for cases after 1875 this is the *United States Supreme Court Reports*, abbreviated *U.S.*), which is preceded by the volume number and followed by the page number:

> The judge ruled that Ms. Warren did have an obligation to offer assistance to the survivors of the wreck, an obligation which she failed to meet (*State of Nevada v. Goldie Warren* 324 U.S. 123).

Before 1875, Supreme Court decisions were published under the names of official court reporters. The reference below is to William Cranch, *Reports of Cases Argued and Adjudged in the Supreme Court of the United States, 1801–1815*, 9 vols. (Washington, DC, 1804–17). The number preceding the clerk's name is the volume number; the last number is the page:

> The first case in which the Supreme Court ruled a law of Congress to be void was *Marbury v. Madison*, in 1803 (1 Cranch 137).

For most of these parenthetical references, it is possible to move some or all of the material outside the parentheses simply by incorporating it in the text:

> In 1969, in *State of Nevada v. Goldie Warren* (324 U.S. 123), the judge ruled that an observer of a traffic accident has an obligation to offer assistance to survivors.

Lower Courts. Decisions of lower federal courts are published in the *Federal Reporter*. The note should give the volume of the *Federal Reporter* (*F.*), the series, if it is other than the first (*2d*, in the model below), the page, and, in brackets, an abbreviated reference to the specific court (the example below is to the Second Circuit Court) and the year:

> One ruling takes into account the bias that often exists against the defendant in certain types of personal injury lawsuits (*United States v. Sizemore*, 183 F.2d 201 [2d Cir. 1950]).

Publications of Government Commissions.   According to *CMS* 14 (15.368), references to bulletins, circulars, reports, and study papers that are issued by various government commissions should include the name of the commission, the date of the document, and the page:

> This year saw a sharp reaction among large firms to the new tax law (Securities and Exchange Commission 2004, 57).

Corporate Authors.   Because government documents are often credited to a corporate author with a lengthy name, you may devise an acronym or a shortened form of the name and indicate in your first reference to the source that this name will be used in later citations:

> Government statistics over the last year showed a continuing leveling of the inflation rate (*Bulletin of Labor Statistics* 2006, 1954; *hereafter BLS*).

The practice of using a shortened name in subsequent references to any corporate author, whether a public or private organization, is sanctioned in most journals, including the *American Political Science Review*, and approved in *CMS* 14 (15.252). Thus, if you refer often to the *U.N. Monthly Bulletin of Statistics*, you may, after giving the publication's full name in the first reference, use a shortened form of the title—perhaps an acronym such as *UNMBS*—in all later cites.

Publications of State and Local Governments.   According to *CMS* 14 (15.377), references to state and local government documents are similar to those for the corresponding national government sources:

> In arguing for the legality of cockfighting, Senator Lynd actually suggested that the "sport" served as a deterrent to crime among the state's young people (Oklahoma Legislature 2004, 24).

■ **Note:** *CMS* 14 (16.178) restricts bibliographical information concerning state laws or municipal ordinances to the running text.

Electronic Sources.   Parenthetical references to electronic sources should present the same sorts of information as references to printed sources, when possible. In other words, include the author's last name, the year of publication, and the relevant page number from the source, if given. However, some types of information that appear in standard text citations, such as the author's name and relevant page numbers, are often missing in electronic sources and so cannot appear in the reference. If the author's name is missing, the parenthetical reference can include the title of the document, in quotation marks. If the online article has numbered paragraphs, you may supply numbers for paragraphs bearing the relevant passages:

> The election results that November may have been what startled Congress into taking such an action ("Effects of Landmark Elections" 2004, para. 12–14).

Interviews.   According to the cms 15 (17.205) *Style Manual*, unpublished interviews should be identified within the text or in a note rather than in a parenthetical citation.

Include in the text the names of the interviewer and the interviewee, the means of communication (whether by telephone, written correspondence, or a formal, face-to-face interview), the date, and, if relevant, the location. If the interview is published, however, it should be given both a text citation and an entry in the reference list at the end of the paper.

Published Interview.

> In an interview last March, Simon criticized the use of private funds to build such city projects as the coliseum (Fox 2005, 58–59).

Unpublished Interview Conducted by the Writer of the Paper.
If you are citing material from an interview that you conducted, you should identify yourself as the author and give the date of the interview:

> In an interview with the author conducted by phone on 23 April 2004, Dr. Kennedy expressed her disappointment with the new court ruling.

Personal Materials. Handle such items as personal email messages and texts from bulletin board discussions within the text instead of in a parenthetical reference. There is no need to provide a citation for such material in the reference list.

5.4 The Author-Date System: Reference List

In a paper using the author-date bibliographic system, the parenthetical references point the reader to the full citations in the reference list. This list, which always follows the text of the paper, is arranged alphabetically according to the first element in each citation. Usually this element is the last name of the author or editor, but in the absence of such information, the citation is alphabetized according to the title of the work, which is then the first element in the citation.

The bibliography is double-spaced throughout, even between entries. As with most alphabetically arranged bibliographies, there is a kind of reverse indentation system called a "hanging indent": after the first line of a citation, all subsequent lines are indented five spaces.

Capitalization. The APSA *Style Manual* uses standard, or "headline style," capitalization rules for titles in the bibliographical citations. In this style, all first and last words in a title, and all other words except articles (*a, an, the*), coordinating words (*and, but, or, for, nor*), and all prepositions, are capitalized.

Books
One Author.

Northrup, Alan K. 2004. *Living High Off the Hog: Recent Pork Barrel Legislation in the Senate*. Cleveland: Johnstown.

First comes the author's name, inverted, then the date of publication, followed by the title of the book, the place of publication, and the name of the publishing house. For place of publication, do not identify the state unless the city is not well known. In that case, use postal abbreviations to denote the state (e.g., *OK, AR*).

Periods are used to divide most of the elements in the citation, although a colon is used between the place of publication and publisher. Custom dictates that the main title and subtitle be separated by a colon, even though a colon may not appear in the title as printed on the title page of the book.

Two Authors.   The name of only the first author is reversed, since it is the one by which the citation is alphabetized:

Spence, Michelle, and Kelly Rudd. 2005. *Education and the Law*. Boston: Tildale.

Three Authors.

Moore, J. B., Jeannine Macrory, and Natasha Traylor. 2004. *Down on the Farm: Renovating the Farm Loan*. Norman: Univ. of Oklahoma Press.

According to *CMS* 15 (17.104), you may abbreviate the word *University* if it appears in the name of the press.

Four or More Authors.

Herring, Ralph, et al. 2004. *Funding City Projects*. Atlanta: Jessup Institute for Policy Development.

Editor, Compiler, or Translator as Author.   When no author is listed on the title page, *CMS* 15 (17.41) calls for you to begin the citation with the name of the editor, compiler, or translator, followed by the appropriate phrase—*ed., comp*, or *trans.*:

Trakas, Dylan, comp. 2004. *Making the Road-Ways Safe: Essays on Highway Preservation and Funding*. El Paso: Del Norte Press.

Editor, Compiler, or Translator with Author.   Place the name of the editor, compiler, or translator after the title, prefaced by the appropriate phrase—*Ed., Comp.*, or *Trans.*:

Pound, Ezra. 1953. *Literary Essays*. Ed. T. S. Eliot. New York: New Directions.

Stomper, Jean. 1973. *Grapes and Rain*. Trans. and ed. John Picard. New York: Baldock.

Two or More Works by the Same Author.   When citing more than one work by the same author or authors, replace the author names in all entries after the first one with a 3-em dash (the equivalent of six hyphens). Arrange the works chronologically by publication date rather than alphabetically by title:

Russell, Henry. 1978. *Famous Last Words: Notable Supreme Court Cases of the Last Five Years*. New Orleans: Liberty Publications.

———, ed. 1988. *Court Battles to Remember*. Denver: Axel & Myers.

Chapter in a Multiauthor Collection.

Gray, Alexa North. 2005. "Foreign Policy and the Foreign Press." In *Current Media Issues*, ed. Barbara Bonnard. New York: Boulanger.

The parenthetical text reference may include the page reference:

(Gray 2005, 191)

If the author and the editor are the same person, you must repeat the name:

Farmer, Susan A. 2004. "Tax Shelters in the New Dispensation: How to Save Your Income." In *Making Ends Meet: Strategies for the Nineties*, ed. Susan A. Farmer. Nashville: Burkette and Hyde.

Author of a Foreword or Introduction.   There is no need, according to *CMS 15* (17.46, 17.74–75), to cite the author of a foreword or introduction in your bibliography, unless you have used material from that author's contribution to the volume. In that case, the bibliography entry is listed under the name of the author of the foreword or introduction. Place the name of the author of the work itself after the title of the work:

Farris, Carla. 2004. Foreword to *Marital Stress and the Professoriat: A Case Study*, by Basil Givan. New York: Galapagos.

The parenthetical text reference cites the name of the author of the foreword or introduction, not the author of the book:

(Farris 2004)

Subsequent Editions.   If you are using an edition of a book other than the first, you must cite the number of the edition or the status, such as *Rev. ed.* for *Revised edition*, if there is no edition number:

Hales, Sarah. 2004. *The Coming Water Wars*. 2d ed. Pittsburgh: Blue Skies.

Multivolume Work.   If you are citing a multivolume work in its entirety, use the following format:

Graybosch, Charles. 1988–89. *The Rise of the Unions*. 3 vols. New York: Starkfield.

If you are citing only one of the volumes in a multivolume work, use the following format:

Ronsard, Madeleine. 2005. *Monopolies*. Vol. 2 of *A History of Capitalism*. Ed. Joseph M. Sayles. Boston: Renfrow.

Reprints.

Adams, Sterling R. [1964] 1988. *How to Win an Election: Promotional Campaign Strategies*. New York: Starkfield.

Modern Editions of Classics.   If the original year of publication is known, include it, in brackets, before the publication date for the edition used:

Burke, Edmond. [1790] 1987. *Reflections on the Revolution in France.* Ed. J. G. A. Pocock. Indianapolis: Hackett.

Remember, if the classic text is divided into short, numbered sections (such as the chapter and verse divisions of the Bible), you do not need to include the work in your bibliography unless you wish to specify a particular edition.

Periodicals
Journal Articles.   Journals are periodicals, usually published either monthly or quarterly, that specialize in serious scholarly articles in a particular field. The revised 2006 edition of the APSA *Style Manual* stipulates that a reference for a journal article must include either the month, the season, or the issue number (in that order of preference), placed just after the volume number.

Hunzecker, Joan. 2004. "Teaching the Toadies: Cronyism in Municipal Politics." *Review of Local Politics* 4 (June): 250–62.

Note that the name of the journal, which is italicized, is followed without punctuation by the volume number. A colon separates the name of the month, in parentheses, from the inclusive page numbers. Do not use *p.* or *pp.* to introduce the page numbers.

Magazine Articles.   Magazines, which are usually published weekly, bimonthly, or monthly, appeal to the popular audience and generally have a wider circulation than journals. *Newsweek* and *Scientific American* are examples of magazines.

Monthly Magazine.   The name of the magazine is separated from the month of publication by a comma:

Stapleton, Bonnie. 1981. "How It Was: On the Campaign Trail with Ike." *Lifetime Magazine*, April, 16–21.

Weekly or Bimonthly Magazine.   The day of the issue's publication appears before the month:

Bruck, Connie. 2006. "The World of Business: A Mogul's Farewell." *The New Californian*, 18 October.

Newspaper Articles.   While the revised 2006 edition of the APSA *Style Manual* does not discuss reference list entries for newspaper articles, *CMS* 15 (15.234–42, 16.117–18) deals with the topic in some detail. Here are two typical models:

New York Times. 2006. Editorial, 10 August.

Fine, Austin. 2010. "Hoag on Trial." *Carrollton (Texas) Tribune*, 24 November.

Note that *The* is omitted from the newspaper's title. If the name of the city in which an American newspaper is published does not appear in the paper's title, it should be appended, in italics. If the city is not well known, the name of the state is added, in italics, in parentheses, as in the second model above.

Public Documents
Congressional Journals.   References to either the *Senate Journal* or the *House Journal* begin with the journal's title and include the years of the session, the number of the Congress and session, and the month and day of the entry:

U.S. Senate Journal. 2006. 105th Cong., 1st sess., 10 December.

The ordinal numbers *second* and *third* may be represented as *d* (52d, 103d) or as *nd* and *rd*, respectively.

Congressional Debates.

Congressional Record.   1930. 72st Cong., 2d sess., vol. 72, pt. 8.

Congressional Reports and Documents.   Following the designation of Senate or House, include as many of the following items as possible, in this order: committee title, year, title of report or document, Congress, session, and report or document number or committee print number.

U.S. Congress. House. Committee on the Budget. 2006. *Report on Government Efficiency As Perceived by the Public*. 105th Cong., 2d sess. H. Rept. 225.

Bills and Resolutions.

U.S. Congress. Senate. 2005. *Visa Formalization Act of 2005*. 105th Cong. 1st sess. S.R. 1437.

The abbreviation *S.R.* in the model above stands for *Senate Resolutions*, and the number following is the bill or resolution number. For references to House bills, the abbreviation is *H.R.*

Statutes.
Citing to the Statutes at Large.

National Flood Insurance Program Enhanced Borrowing Authority Act. 2006. *U. S. Statutes at Large*. Vol. 120, p. 317.

Citing to the U.S. Code.

National Flood Insurance Program Enhanced Borrowing Authority Act. 2006. *U. S. Code*. Vol. 42, sec. 4001.

United States Constitution.   While the revised 2006 edition of the APSA *Style Manual* does not discuss references for the U.S. Constitution, *CMS* 14 (16.172) states that the Constitution is not listed in the bibliography.

Executive Department Documents.   Include the name of the corporate author, the year, title, city, and publisher:

Department of Labor. 2004. *Report on Urban Growth Potential Projections.*
     Washington, DC: GPO.

The abbreviation for the publisher in the above model, GPO, stands for the *Government Printing Office*, which prints and distributes most government publications. According to *CMS* 15 (15.327), you may use any of the following formats to refer to the GPO:

Washington, DC: U.S. Government Printing Office, 2005
Washington, DC: Government Printing Office, 2005
Washington, DC: GPO, 2005
Washington, DC, 2005

Remember to be consistent in using the form you choose.

Legal References.
Supreme Court.   Use the same format as for the parenthetical text citation, only add the date after the name of the case:

State of Nevada v. Goldie Warren. 1969. 324 U.S. 123.

For a case prior to 1875, use the following format:

Marbury v. Madison. 1803. 1 Cranch 137.

Lower Courts.   Include the volume of the *Federal Reporter* (F.), the series, if it is other than the first (*2d*, in the model below), the page, and, in parentheses, an abbreviated reference to the specific district.

United States v. Sizemore. 1950. 183 F.2d 201 (2d Cir.).

Publications of Government Commissions.

U.S. Securities and Exchange Commission. 1984. *Annual Report of the Securities and Exchange Commission for the Fiscal Year.* Washington, DC: GPO.

Publications of State and Local Governments.   Remember that references for state and local government publications are modeled on those for corresponding national government documents:

Oklahoma Legislature. 2006. Joint Committee on Public Recreation. *Final Report to the Legislature, 2006, Regular Session, on Youth Activities.* Oklahoma City.

Electronic Sources.   If a source is available in both print and electronic forms, it is preferable to use the print form. But if you have used the electronic version and it is different from the print version, the general practice is to make your reference to the electronic source as similar as possible to that for the print version, adding the full retrieval path (the electronic address) and the date of your last access of the material.

Electronic Book.   Begin with the author's name, reversed, followed if possible by date of publication, then the title of the work, the retrieval path, and the date of your last access to the work, in parentheses.

Amshiral, Sretas. 2004. *Aviation in the Far East*. http://www.flight_easthist.org (January 3, 2005).

Chapter in an Electronic Book.

Burris, Akasha. 2004. "Experiments in Transubstantiation." *Surviving Global Disaster*. http://www.meekah/exit/paleoearth.html (March 5, 2005).

You may continue a lengthy URL on the next line of the reference. Do not add a hyphen at the end of the first line.

Electronic Journals.   Include all of the following information that you can find, in this order: name of author, reversed; year of publication; title of article, in quotation marks; title of journal, in italics; any further publication information, such as volume number, day or month; full retrieval path; and date of your last access, in parentheses:

Zoheret, Jeanie. 2003. "The Politics of Social Deprivation." *B & N Digest* 3 (February). http://postmodern/tsu/b&n.edu (December 5, 2004).

Material from a Website.   The author's name (reversed) and year of publication are followed by the title of the article, in quotation marks; the title, if applicable, of the complete work or Web page, in italics; the full Web address (URL); and, finally, the date on which you last accessed the page, in parentheses:

Squires, Lawrence. 2004. "A Virtual Tour of the White House, circa 1900." *National Landmarks: Then and Now*. http://www.natlandmk.com/hist (August 21, 2004).

E-Mail Material.   The revised 2006 edition of the APSA *Style Manual* suggests that e-mail, bulletin board, and electronic discussion group messages be cited as personal communication in the text and left out of the reference list.

Interviews
Published Interview.

Untitled Interview in a Book.

Jorgenson, Mary. 2004. Interview by Alan McAskill. In *Hospice Pioneers*. Ed. Alan McAskill, 62–86. Richmond: Dynasty Press.

Titled Interview in a Periodical.

Simon, John. 2004. "Picking the Patrons Apart: An Interview with John Simon." By Selena Fox. *Media Week*, March 14, 40–46.

Interview on Television.

Snopes, Edward. 2004. Interview by Klint Gordon. *Oklahoma Politicians*. WKY Television, 4 June.

Unpublished Interview.   According to *CMS* 15 (17.208), unpublished interviews should be identified within the running text or in a note rather than in a parenthetical citation and left out of the reference list.

Unpublished Sources.
Theses and Dissertations.   If the work has a sewn or glued binding, place the title in italics, like a book; otherwise designate the title by quotation marks:

Hoarner, Art. 2005. *Populism and the Free Soil Movement*. Ph.D. diss. University of Virginia.

Sharpe, Ellspeth Stanley. 2003. "Black Women in Politics: A Troubled History." Master's thesis. Oregon State University.

Paper Presented at a Meeting.

Zelazny, Kim, and Ed Gilmore. 2005. "Art for Art's Sake: Funding the NEA in the Twenty-First Century." Presented at the Annual Meeting of the Conference of Metropolitan Arts Councils, San Francisco.

Manuscript in the Author's Possession.

Borges, Rita V. 1979. "Mexican-American Border Conflicts, 1915–1970." University of Texas at El Paso. Photocopy.

The entry includes the institution with which the author is affiliated and ends with a description of the format of the work (typescript, photocopy, etc.).

Personal Communications.   Handle such items as personal email messages and texts from bulletin board discussions within the text or in a note instead of in a parenthetical reference. There is no need to provide a citation for such material in the reference list.

■ **Note:** Most of the sources used as models in this chapter are not references to actual publications.

Sample Bibliography: APSA Author-Date System

Ariès, Philippe. 1962. *Centuries of Childhood: A Social History of Family Life*. Trans. Robert Baldock. New York: Knopf.

Cesbron, Henry. 1909. *Histoire critique de l'hystérie*. Paris: Asselin et Houzeau.

Farmer, Susan A. 2004. "Tax Shelters in the New Dispensation: How to Save Your Income." In *Making Ends Meet: Strategies for the Nineties*, ed. Susan A. Farmer. Nashville: Burkette and Hyde.

Herring, Ralph, et al. 2004. *Funding City Projects*. Atlanta: Jessup Institute for Policy Development.

Hunzecker, Joan. 2004. "Teaching the Toadies: Cronyism in Municipal Politics." *Review of Local Politics* 4:250–62.

Moore, J. B., Jeannine Macrory, and Natasha Traylor. 2004. *Down on the Farm: Renovating the Farm Loan*. Norman: Univ. of Oklahoma Press.

Northrup, Alan K. 2004. *Living High Off the Hog: Recent Pork Barrel Legislation in the Senate*. Cleveland: Johnstown.

Skylock, Browning. 1991. "'Fifty-Four Forty or Fight!': Sloganeering in Early America." *American History Digest* 28(3): 25–34.

Squires, Lawrence. 2006. "A Virtual Tour of the White House, circa 1900." *National Landmarks: Then and Now*. http://www.natlandmk. com/hist (21 August 2004).

Stapleton, Bonnie. 1981. "How It Was: On the Campaign Trail with Ike." *Lifetime Magazine*, April.

U.S. Securities and Exchange Commission. 1984. *Annual Report of the Securities and Exchange Commission for the Fiscal Year*. Washington, 2005.

5.5   Avoid Plagiarism

You want to use your source material as effectively as possible. This will sometimes mean that you should quote from a source directly, whereas at other times you will want to express such information in your own words. At all times, you should work to integrate the source material skillfully into the flow of your written argument.

When to Quote

You should quote directly from a source when the original language is distinctive enough to enhance your argument, or when rewording the passage would lessen its impact. In the interest of fairness, you should also quote a passage to which you will take exception. Rarely, however, should you quote a source at great length (longer than two or three paragraphs). Nor should your paper, or any substantial section of it, be merely a string of quoted passages. The more language you take from the writings of others, the more the quotations will disrupt the rhetorical flow of your own words. Too much quoting creates a choppy patchwork of varying styles and borrowed purposes in which your sense of your own control over your material is lost.

Quotations in Relation to Your Writing

When you do use a quotation, make sure that you insert it skillfully. According to *CMS* 15 (11.11-12), quotations of fewer than 100 words (approximately eight typed lines) should generally be integrated into the text and set off with quotation marks:

> "In the last analysis," Alice Thornton argued in 2006, "we cannot afford not to embark on a radical program of fiscal reform" (12).

A quotation of 100 words or longer (eight typed lines or longer) should be formatted as a *block quotation*; it should begin on a new line, be indented from the left margin, and not be enclosed in quotation marks.

> Blake's outlook for the solution to the city's problem of abandoned buildings is anything but optimistic:
>
> > If the trend in demolitions due to abandonment continues, the cost of doing nothing may be too high. The three-year period from 2004 to 2007 shows an annual increase in demolitions of roughly twenty percent. Such an upward trend for a sustained period of time would eventually place a disastrous hardship on the city's resources. And yet the city council seems bent on following the tactic of inaction. (2004, 8)

Acknowledge Quotations Carefully

Failing to signal the presence of a quotation skillfully can lead to confusion or choppiness:

> The U.S. Secretary of Labor believes that worker retraining programs have failed because of a lack of trust within the American business culture. "The American business community does not visualize the need to invest in its workers" (Winn 2004, 11).

The first sentence in the above passage seems to suggest that the quote that follows comes from the Secretary of Labor. Note how this revision clarifies the attribution:

> According to reporter Fred Winn, the U.S. Secretary of Labor believes that worker retraining programs have failed because of a lack of trust within the American business culture. Summarizing the secretary's view, Winn writes, "The American business community does not visualize the need to invest in its workers" (2004, 11).

The origin of each quote must be indicated within your text at the point where the quote occurs as well as in the list of works cited, which follows the text.

Quote Accurately

If your transcription of a quotation introduces careless variants of any kind, you are misrepresenting your source. Proofread your quotations very carefully, paying close attention to such surface features as spelling, capitalization, italics, and the use of numerals.

Occasionally, in order to make a quotation fit smoothly into a passage, to clarify a reference, or to delete unnecessary material, you may need to change the original wording slightly. You must, however, signal any such change to your reader. Some alterations may be noted by brackets:

> "Several times in the course of his speech, the attorney general said that his stand [on gun control] remains unchanged" (McAffrey 2004, 2).

Ellipses indicate that words have been left out of a quote:

"The last time voters refused to endorse one of the senator's policies . . . was back in 1982" (Laws 2005, 143).

When you integrate quoted material with your own prose, it is unnecessary to begin the quote with ellipses:

Benton raised eyebrows with his claim that "nobody in the mayor's office knows how to tie a shoe, let alone balance a budget" (Williams 2006, 12).

Paraphrasing

Your writing has its own rhetorical attributes, its own rhythms and structural coherence. Inserting several quotations into one section of your paper can disrupt the patterns of your prose and diminish its effectiveness. Paraphrasing, or recasting source material in your own words, is one way to avoid the choppiness that can result from a series of quotations.

Remember that a paraphrase is to be written in your language; it is not a near-copy of the source writer's language. Merely changing a few words of the original does justice to no one's prose and frequently produces stilted passages. This sort of borrowing is actually a form of plagiarism. To integrate another's material into your own writing fully, use your own language.

Paraphrasing may actually increase your comprehension of source material, because in recasting a passage you will have to think very carefully about its meaning—more carefully, perhaps, than if you had merely copied it word for word.

Avoiding Plagiarism When Paraphrasing

Paraphrases require the same sort of documentation as direct quotes. The words of a paraphrase may be yours, but the idea belongs to someone else. Failure to give that person credit, in the form of references within the text and in the bibliography, may make you vulnerable to a charge of plagiarism.

Plagiarism is the use of someone else's words or ideas without proper credit. Although some plagiarism is deliberate, produced by writers who understand that they are guilty of a kind of academic thievery, much of it is unconscious, committed by writers who are not aware of the varieties of plagiarism or who are careless in recording their borrowings from sources. Plagiarism includes:

- Quoting directly without acknowledging the source
- Paraphrasing without acknowledging the source
- Constructing a paraphrase that closely resembles the original in language and syntax

One way to guard against plagiarism is to keep careful notes of when you have directly quoted source material and when you have paraphrased—making sure that the wording of the paraphrases is yours. Be sure that all direct quotes in your final draft are properly set off from your own prose, either with quotation marks or in indented blocks.

What kind of paraphrased material must be acknowledged? Basic material that you find in several sources need not be documented by a reference. For example, it is unnecessary to cite a source for the information that Franklin Delano Roosevelt was elected to a fourth term as president of the United States shortly before his death, because this is a commonly known fact. However, Professor Smith's opinion, published in a recent article, that Roosevelt's winning of a fourth term hastened his death is not a fact, but a theory based on Smith's research and defended by her. If you wish to use Smith's opinion in a paraphrase, you need to credit her, as you should all judgments and claims from another source. Any information that is not widely known, whether factual or open to dispute, should be documented. This includes statistics, graphs, tables, and charts taken from sources other than your own primary research.

Part II
Warm-Up: Critical Thinking About Politics and Government

CHAPTER 6

Writing to Communicate and Act

6.1   Write a Letter to Your Local Newspaper Editor

A letter to a newspaper editor is neither an exercise in creative writing nor a philosophical thought piece. Its audience is not the editor so much as the general public, for your goal in writing the letter is to get it published in the newspaper so that you can influence the opinions of others. Because your aim is publication, remember that most letters that are actually published are responses to a specific editorial, article, or letter that has already (and recently) appeared in the paper. Successful letters to the editor, therefore, are well written statements that

- Point out and then correct inaccurate, false, or misleading information in a recently printed news item, editorial, or letter
- Supplement, reinforce, refute, or clarify a recently printed statement with new information
- Offer a new point of view on a current issue or a recently printed statement

How Do I Find a Topic?

On the shelves of the periodicals room of your college library you can find the last several issues of your local newspaper. Read through them, looking for articles or other items that particularly interest you. Can you find something that you feel passionate about? Pay special attention to letters to the editor. Note the types of letters that the newspaper is printing. Are they long or short? Are they well balanced, or do they tend to be incendiary? Find a specific news article, editorial, or letter to the editor that interests you personally and that you believe is of interest to people in your community. Examine the article carefully. What point is it trying to make? What are the article's strengths and weaknesses? Did the author of the article leave out something important? What do you have to say about the issue at hand? Do you have any new ideas? Identify one or two specific points that you would like to make about the issue in general and specifically about the published article you are writing about. Do not attempt to address every issue in the article you have selected, only one or two of the major ones.

How Do I Go About Writing the Letter?

Start by preparing an outline of the points you want to make in your letter (see Chapter 1, pages 20–21, for tips on constructing an outline). You should make no more than three major points, and one or two is better. You will, however, need to support your point(s) with persuasive argument, facts, and a clear explanation of the issue you are addressing. It is imperative to make your point clearly and immediately, and only then go on to defend it. It is a good practice, therefore, to have your thesis sentence (see Chapter 1, page 13, for a discussion of the thesis sentence) be the first sentence in the letter. Your thesis sentence is the main point you are trying to make. Either in or immediately after the thesis sentence, identify the article or editorial to which you are responding.

After your thesis sentence, present a concise, logical argument for the point you are making. Some other considerations are worthy of thought. Letters that sound too extreme are less likely to be effective than those that appear thoughtful and balanced. Be sure to write the letter so that it stands on its own, that is, the reader can understand it without having to read other materials. One more thing: Letters do not always have to be critical. It is often helpful to be as positive as possible, pointing out the competencies and successes of others.

The Importance of Correctness

Have you ever read something—an article, a billboard, or an ad in a paper—trying to convince you to take a particular action ("vote for me," "eat at Joe's") and found a glaring grammar error? "You're future is safe with Senator Smith." What does it do to your confidence in the argument being made to find that its writer is careless in this way? Most people find their attention going to the error, their focus deflected into rumination on the intelligence or education of the person who wrote or copied the offending text. It may not seem fair to you, but it is a fact: simple mistakes in your text can devastate your argument. In the case of a letter to the editor, a single typo or grammar error—"hat" instead of "has," "it's" instead of "its"—may be so off-putting to the editorial staff that your letter gets filed in the wastebasket rather than published.

Proofread.   The format of your letter is important. You should use a standard business letter format. Most of them call for single spacing the text and the various addresses, double spacing only between paragraphs and between elements of the letter. In addition, look in the newspaper's editorial section and you will probably find specific directions and policies for submitting letters. Type your letter on good quality paper. Address the letter to the Editor of the newspaper. Include your name, address, phone number, and e-mail address. The newspaper may check to be sure you are who you claim to be. After you write the letter, send it immediately so it will be fresh and pertinent. Check the paper daily to see if it has been printed. After a week, if you have not had a reply, send a follow-up letter to check your letter's status.

Sample Letter to the Editor

September 10, 2011
Mildred K. Feswick
Editor
Freetown Daily News
P.O., Box 2367
Freetown, TX 05672

Dear Ms. Feswick:

Education is the cornerstone of our society and deserves much more public support than it is currently getting. In an editorial that appeared on page 10 of the Freetown Daily News on Thursday, September 8, you stated "The Federal government spends too much money on education." I hope you will reconsider your opinion.

First, consider the impressive and pervasive value of education. The acquisition of knowledge is beneficial not only for the personal satisfaction that comes from learning about yourself and your culture, but for the resulting intellectual contributions to society as well. Statistics show that educated people make better decisions and contribute more to society than uneducated people do. National statistics clearly demonstrate the effectiveness of an education. College graduates have an unemployment rate that is half that of high school graduates and the median income of a college graduate is $15,000 greater than the income of a high school graduate. Despite the effectiveness of these programs and the stunning statistics they produce, the government insists on cutting back on educational spending.

Parents are aware of the opportunities and insight a good education provides. In a recent poll, 98 percent of parents in America said they wanted their children to attend college. However, it is becoming increasingly difficult for parents to finance that education. Pell grants, which originally funded up to 75 percent of a student's education, now fund only up to 25 percent. Studies show that federal student aid programs have been extremely effective at educating people who otherwise could not have afforded college. Despite clear evidence that education is a good investment, it is not high on many legislators' lists of priorities. Funding for public schools and higher education is diminishing in the wake of excessive spending on other programs. For example, a report recently issued by the Justice Policy Institute, a research and advocacy organization in Washington, DC, reveals that California and Florida now spend more money on prisons than on higher education. The report also says the average cost to incarcerate a felon is from $22,000 to $25,000 per year, the same amount charged by selective liberal arts colleges. If we can pay large sums of money to keep people from being productive, we should be able to find the funds to help people lead more productive and fulfilling lives.

President Bush had spearheaded the effort to slash educational appropriations programs. Rather than providing sufficient funds for public schools, his "No Child Left Behind" program withdraws funds from schools that do not meet federal standards. This policy might be reasonable if schools had adequate funding to begin with, but they don't. Many of the nation's teachers pay for school supplies out of their own pockets.

Education is the key to our country's economic future. We have the world's strongest economy because our educational institutions lead the world in producing competent graduates. It is therefore easy to see that the statement "The federal government spends too much money on education" is refuted by a thoughtful analysis of the benefits of federal aid to education. The comparatively small amount of money set aside for education is a clear indication of our country's lack of concern for our future. Today education is more important than ever. Our potential will go unmet unless we invest in properly training our minds. Education is the catalyst of a successful future.

Sincerely,

Jeremy M. Scott
3251 Matlock Road #22
Mansfield, TX 76063

6.2   Submit an Op-ed Essay

An *op-ed essay* is a statement of perspective on an issue or matter of concern to the community that normally appears on the page of the newspaper opposite the editorial page (hence, "op-ed"). It is neither an editorial (written by the newspaper editor) nor a letter to the editor (most often responding to an article or editorial previously published). Instead, it is a carefully formulated and engagingly written attention-grabbing essay that is intended primarily to stimulate thinking on part of newspaper readers with the ultimate goal of influencing their opinions. Unlike letters to the editor, an op-ed essay is often both an exercise in creative writing and a philosophical thought piece. Like letters to the editor, an op-ed's audience is the general public. Successful (published) op-ed essays usually display some or all of the following characteristics:

- A radical, incendiary, or at least distinctive point of view
- A new angle on a common topic
- A consistent, coherent theme
- Facts and anecdotes
- Humor or satire

How Do I Find a Topic?

Begin your topic search in the same manner you look for a topic for a letter to the editor. On the shelves of the periodicals room of your college library you can find the last several issues of your local newspaper. Read through them, looking for articles or other items that particularly interest you. Can you find something that you feel passionate about? Pay special attention to the op-ed pieces you find. Notice their subjects, styles, and approaches to issues. Pay special attention to their length. Find an issue that interests you personally and that you believe is of interest to people in your community. Identify one or two specific points that you would like to make about the issue.

How Do I Go About Writing the Op-ed Essay?

As you would with a letter to the editor, start by preparing an outline of the points you want to make in your essay (see Chapter 1, pages 20–21, for tips on constructing an outline). You should make no more than three major points in your essay. You will need to support your point(s) with persuasive argument, facts, and a clear explanation of the issue you are addressing. It is imperative to clearly and immediately make your point, and only then go on to defend it. It is a good practice, therefore, to make your thesis sentence the first sentence in the essay (see Chapter 1, page 13, for a discussion of the thesis sentence). Your thesis sentence is the main point you are trying to make.

After your thesis sentence, present a concise, logical argument for your point. Some other considerations are worthy of thought. Although op-ed pieces are often more radical in viewpoint than letters to the editor, an essay that simply thrashes at people or presents an unending stream of sarcasm is unlikely to be effective—or published. You may be dramatic to engage the reader, but be sure also to make a well-reasoned and well-documented argument. Be sure to write the essay so that it stands on its own, that is, so that the reader can understand it without reading other materials. Do not forget to proofread and check for spelling and grammar errors. As with letters to the editor, careful proofreading is absolutely essential to the success of your op-ed piece.

The format of your essay is important. You should format the essay as you would a college term paper. In addition, look in the newspaper's editorial section and you will probably find specific directions and policies for submitting op-ed essays. Type your essay on good quality paper. Include a cover letter to the editor citing your name, address, phone number, and e-mail address. The newspaper may check to be sure you are who you claim to be. Check the paper daily to see if your essay has been printed. After a week, if you have not had a reply, send a follow-up letter to check your essay's status.

You will find current examples of op-ed essays in your local newspaper or in the *New York Times* online.

6.3   Write to Your Representative or Senator

Elected representatives, especially members of the U.S. Senate and House of Representatives, receive scores of letters every day. Although you may write to wish your senator a happy birthday or complain about the senator's wardrobe, most letters to elected representatives are for two purposes: (1) to influence her or him to vote a certain way on an issue that is currently being considered before the legislature or (2) to request that some member of the representative's staff perform a specific service, such as providing information or helping solve a problem encountered with a government agency. You may write a letter on any matter you please, but the goal of this particular assignment is to help you write the former type, that is, a letter that requests a representative to vote a certain way on impending legislation.

Letters to representatives are most likely to be influential when they are persuasively written and when they represent the view of a constituent. Your letter, therefore, should be addressed to your own senator or representative, and you should view it primarily as an exercise in persuasion. Letters that influence the votes of legislators often have several characteristics. First, they are brief and concise. Elected officials are very busy and, because they take in an immense amount of information each day, have very little patience for long-winded epistles that fail to get to the point. Second, good letters clearly identify a single action that their authors want the representative to take, stating and justifying the need for the requested action. Finally, good letters that concern a bill currently before Congress letter provide a brief summary of what the bill does. This may seem unnecessary, but Congress considers hundreds of bills each year, and often several appear simultaneously to address the same issue. You will want to save the representative some time by explaining exactly what she or he will be voting for.

How Do I Find a Topic?

The best place to start is THOMAS (http://thomas.loc.gov/), the home page of the Library of Congress, which provides online search engines and texts for all current legislation. Think of a topic in which you have a personal interest. Are you majoring in nursing? You may want to examine current legislation related to health care. Are you a music lover? Is any legislation passing that affects the music industry or your access to music on the Internet? Is there an issue pending that affects your personal congressional district? Whatever your interest, identify one or two key works and enter them into the THOMAS legislation search engine. You will then be presented a list of legislation in which your search terms are mentioned. After you locate a bill currently being considered by Congress that interests you, use the THOMAS Congressional Record search engine, enter the name of the bill, and you will find a record of speeches that have been made in Congress for and against the measure in question. Next, decide whether you are for or against the legislation and write down an initial list of your reasons for supporting or opposing it.

How Do I Go About Writing the Letter?

First, address your letter properly. A table providing proper forms of address is printed at the end of this section of this chapter. Begin your letter by telling the representative exactly what you want him or her to do and which piece of legislation is affected. Be sure to include the following information, which you will find when you locate the bill in the online *Congressional Digest:*

- Name of the bill (e.g., Environmental Justice Act of 2011)
- Subtitle of the bill (e.g., "an act to require federal agencies to develop and implement policies and practices that promote environmental justice, and for other purposes")
- Bill's number (e.g., H. R. 2200)
- Current status of the bill (e.g., referred to the Subcommittee on Commercial and Administrative Law)

Next, address two of the legislator's primary concerns. For every bill that comes to the representative's attention, he or she must answer two questions: (1) Is legislative action needed to deal with whatever problem or issue is at hand? and (2) If legislation is needed, is the specific legislation in question the best way to address the issue? To answer these two questions you will need to make the following two arguments: (1) That the issue or problem warrants (or does not warrant) legislative action and (2) that the specific proposed legislation appropriately deals (or does not appropriately deal) with the issue or problem.

Provide at least a few facts and examples or anecdotes. Include any personal experience or involvement that you have in the issue or problem. You do not need to provide all the information the legislator will need to make a decision, but provide enough to get her or him interested in the issue enough to examine the matter further and give it serious thought. Format the letter as you do a standard business letter and, of course, proofread your final draft carefully. You will find a table of proper forms of address for letters to government officials in Appendix B of this Manual.

Sample Letter to a Representative

October 5, 2011
The Honorable Stephanie Herseth
1504 Longworth House Office Building
Washington, DC, 20515

Dear Representative Herseth:

I am writing to ask you to vote for the Environmental Justice Act of 2011 (H. R. 2200, currently under consideration by the Subcommittee on Commercial and Administrative Law), an act "To require Federal agencies to develop and implement policies and practices that promote environmental justice, and for other purposes." Native Americans, Latinos, and Blacks have suffered too long under unhealthy environmental conditions on reservations and in substandard neighborhoods across the country. In my neighborhood the toxic waste from old mining operations has caused illness in more than twenty children.

Across the country Superfund sites and pockets of polluted air and water are affecting most the people with the fewest resources and the least political clout to deal with the problem. In Los Angeles, for example, more than 70 percent of African-Americans and half of Latinos reside in the most highly polluted areas while only a third of the local whites live in these areas. Again, workers in the meatpacking plants of South Omaha, Nebraska, are battling to restore the vitality of city parks and improve unsanitary conditions in the plants. Too often people in these communities face greater exposure to toxins and dangerous substances because waste dumps, industrial facilities, and chemical storage facilities take fewer precautions in low-income communities than they do in high-income communities. Sadly, the captains of industry view these communities as expendable, denying the human beings who live in them the dignity and respect that is their constitutional right as American citizens.

What can be done? The first step is to solve a problem in and among federal agencies. Recent environmental and health policy studies have determined that most federal agencies, including the Environmental Protection Agency, do not adequately understand that environmental justice is being continuously denied to American citizens. Furthermore, there is currently no mechanism in place to coordinate and therefore make effective the environmental justice efforts that are currently under way.

The Environmental Justice Act of 2008 does much to correct these problems. In addition to focusing federal agency attention on the environmental and human health conditions in minority, low-income, and Native American communities, this legislation takes several positive steps in the direction of securing environmental justice for Native Americans. It

- Ensures that all federal agencies develop practices that promote environmental justice
- Increases cooperation and coordination among federal agencies
- Provides minority, low-income, and Native American communities greater access to public information and opportunity for participation in environmental decision-making
- Mitigates the inequitable distribution of the burdens and benefits of federal programs having significant impact on human health and the environment
- Holds federal agencies accountable for the effects of their projects and programs on all communities.

Your support in this urgent matter is much appreciated.

Sincerely,

P. Charles Longbranch III
18 Lake Charles Way
Passamadumcott, SD 57003

6.4   Contribute to a Political Blog

When British Petroleum's drilling rig Deepwater Horizon exploded in the Gulf of Mexico in April 2010, it created the largest oil spill in the nation's history and generated weeks of controversy. Dr. Kurt Hochenauer, political blogger and Professor of English at the University of Central Oklahoma, wasted no time diving into the cold political waters that ensued. His own blog, *Okie Funk: Notes From the Outback*, had won the Oklahoma Blogging Association's Best Political (Liberal) Blog Award for 2009. A banner on his blogsite (okiefunk.com) reads "This is a blog of populist and liberal information and ideas, advancing the cause of truth and justice while fighting the ugly tyranny of right-wing oppression in Oklahoma and its surrounding environs." These are fighting words in the reddest state in the nation. (Oklahoma was the only state in which every single county voted Republican in the 2008 presidential election.) Annoyed with what he perceived was an attempt by conservatives to use the spill to attack President Obama, Hochenauer (dochoc) fired back with this posting on May 30, 2010.

False Comparison

In 2005, more than 1,800 people died in Hurricane Katrina, which flooded 80 percent of New Orleans, causing epic proportions of destruction and displacing thousands of people.

Many suffering people thought the government's immediate response to the hurricane's aftermath in New Orleans was not quick enough, and former President George Bush was widely criticized for not realizing the scope of the disaster until later. Those are simply nonpartisan facts. People still disagree on whether Bush deserved the criticism or not.

It's important to keep these facts in mind as Republicans try to spin the British Petroleum oil spill in the Gulf of Mexico near Louisiana as President Barack Obama's "Katrina." The initial explosion on the ocean oil platform killed 11 people, which is tragic, but it's not anywhere close to 1,800 deaths. No one has been displaced. No homes or schools have been destroyed. There are not thousands upon thousands of people suffering in the heat without water or food. The federal government is doing everything it can to stop the leak in conjunction with BP, which is going to pay for the cleanup.

In fact, the leak, which is causing an environmental disaster, can on one level be attributed to the GOP-backed philosophy of drilling for oil wherever it can be found despite the consequences on the environment. It can also be attributed to market fundamentalism, another piece of GOP ideology, which supports deregulation and fewer government restrictions on businesses like oil companies. I'm not arguing that there are no Democrats who support these positions, but market fundamentalism—the idea that markets will correct errors on their own without government intervention—has been a mainstay of Republican ideology.

The loss of lives on the oil platform is tragic and the spill is creating an environmental disaster, but to compare it to Katrina is to minimize what happened in 2005. It's just an obvious political ploy to distort the underlying causes of the spill and to deflect attention away from GOP "drill, baby, drill" sloganeering. The leak, which some experts say has spewed as much as 39 million gallons of oil into the ocean, shows this country needs to turn to renewable, alternative energy sources as quickly as possible. That's the real story of the spill, a story the GOP wants to hide with a pointless, absurd comparison.

Obama is not responsible for decades of deregulation and corporate favoritism. He's not responsible for the fact the country needs to have better public transportation systems so Americans will use less oil. He didn't invent the SUV.

The spill is not Obama's Katrina; it's the culmination of harmful political ideologies that place corporate profits above anything else.

Do you *feel* anything when you read Hochenauer's post? Anger against Republicans? Anger against Hochenauer? If you are inclined to react, one way or another, you are experiencing one of the fundamental effects of good blogging: emotion. In a world in which hundreds of thousands of blog posts are created each day, a blogger's first goal is to get noticed.

Let's back up a bit for some basics, to make sure we are all on the same page. Only a few years ago blogs (web-logs) were simple forums for exchanging ideas. Now they are much more than that. Although they are still often used simply to banter thoughts, blogs have become weapons for political warfare. Through blogs, candidates, parties, and political movements can formulate, clarify, and define political objectives and strategies. They can be powerful tools for gaining and organizing support.

A *post* is a comment added to a blog. Most posts have a subject line (header) that announces the author and topic of the comment that follows. They are usually listed in order of time posted, starting with the most recent and proceeding to the oldest. There are thousands of blogs and millions of posts. You can Google them and follow the directions you find to post your comments. The purpose of the discussion you are currently reading is to get you to think about what you are going to say so that you may contribute more *persuasively*. Some blogs are created purely for entertainment, and that is perfectly fine, but it is not what we are after in our efforts to learn how to participate in politics. Think about it. As you read through the headers in a political blog, which posts are you likely select to read if you actually want to learn something? Which posts draw you into a meaningful discussion, ones with empty rants, or ones that provide you the opportunity to engage in a substantive discussion of an issue that interest you? We hope you will choose the latter.

With that in mind, we offer some simple guidelines for contributing to a blog.

1. Pick a current topic that interests you. Most successful posts are written by people who know something about what they are saying, and they know what they know because they have been learning about it for some time. Leslie Goldman, who

blogs on Huffpost (Arianna Huffington's blog site), advises you to "Blog your passion." Just go online to your favorite news source (hopefully one that is respected for its accuracy) and keep reading until something pushes an internal button.

2. Take the time to choose a good blog. For the purpose of learning something about politics, a good blog (1) contains a high proportion of earnest political discussion, (2) includes informed opinions as opposed to empty rhetoric, (3) includes entries which indicate that a discussion is actually evolving. Ideas become more perceptive and informed as helpful comments are added to the discussion. You can choose a blog with an obvious bias, like Dr. Hochenauer's, either because you share his views or want to challenge them, or you can choose a more neutral blog. In either case, whether the discussion is heated or not, participate where people are honest and respectful of each other, even when they strongly disagree.

3. Think before you write. As you read through various posts you will find that some authors have more interesting, informative, and engaging things to say than others. Your goal is to be a contributor who is popular and influential. This means that, even though blogging gains much of its vitality and usefulness from the speed with which contributors respond, you still need to take care to say exactly what you want to say in exactly the way you want to say it. You may, for example, want to compose your contribution in a word processing program like Word rather than on the email response page, since a wrong keystroke made halfway through the writing of a posting can send your message out to the world before it is ready to get there. By adding the extra step of transferring your text, when it is finished, from one program to another, you may also be giving yourself the time and the inclination to revise a bit more thoroughly than you might do if you compose on the same page from which you will launch your posting.

4. Join the conversation. Get into the flow of what is being said. Listen carefully to what others are saying and respond to something that is being said. If you want to attack something, attack ideas or behaviors, not people. Libel leaves you open to a lawsuit, even in a blog. Dr. Hochenauer's post does not defame the character of individuals. It attacks the ideas and tactics of a political party.

5. Have something interesting and new to say. Add original observations to the discussion. Facts normally speak more convincingly than opinions. You may want to research the topic you select. Find out whether or not what other bloggers say is true. Find credible sources of information and put them to work. People who have something to say about everything are rarely influential about anything. If you have the wit and talent of Jon Stewart or Stephen Colbert, then you may have great success if you dive blindly in. Most of us, however, have noticed that people who offer a limited number of astute comments are more interesting than those who talk a lot about everything. Remember to respect copyright laws. Quote only short portions of work unless you have permission from the author to do otherwise and cite the sources of your information unless it is common knowledge. The blog post printed above is included in this Manual with Dr. Hochenauer's permission.

6. Write an eye-catching header. The header "False Comparison," for example, tends to make you ask questions. What is the comparison? Why is it false?

7. Be brief and concise. Clearly identify a single point and make it with punch and power. Humor is helpful if it adds rather than detracts from the point you are trying to make. A good general rule is to write what you want to say, and then cut it in half. In other words, say the same thing in half as many words as in your original draft contains.

8. As you continue to blog, generate your own personal, effective style, constructing arguments that are well-phrased, valid, and cogent. And be sure to avoid the logical fallacies that appear in much if not most expressed opinion. The purpose of sections 2.3 and 2.4 of this manual is to help you with these tasks. Follow the basic pattern of the short essay: (1) clearly state your main point, (2) write a sufficient number of paragraphs explaining and supporting your point, and (3) provide a strong conclusion that ties the essay together. Study the structure of Hochenauer's blog, which uses this pattern effectively.

CHAPTER 7
Write to Analyze Politics or Government Policy

7.1   Analyze a Campaign Commercial

The Ghost of Willie Horton

It's a classic and infamous television campaign ad. A foreboding prison tower, somber and gray, sharply cuts through a gloomy stillness. The camera focuses on a rifle-toting guard patrolling a barbed-wire-topped wall. Next, marching in file, monochrome prisoners enter a revolving door that places them momentarily inside the prison, but then sweeps them immediately out to freedom. As the line of prisoners continues its bizarre liberation, the following banners sequentially appear on the screen:

> The Dukakis Furlough Program
> 268 escaped
> Many are still at large

Meanwhile, a resonant voice intones: "As governor, Michael Dukakis vetoed mandatory sentences for drug dealers. He vetoed the death penalty. His revolving door prison policy gave weekend furloughs to first-degree murderers not eligible for parole. While out, many committed other crimes like kidnapping and rape. And many are still at large. Now Michael Dukakis says he wants to do for America what he's done for Massachusetts. America can't afford that risk."

It's all over in 30 seconds, and it's one of the most famous campaign ads in history. Having spent eight years as Ronald Reagan's Vice President, George Herbert Walker Bush was eager to retain Republican control in the 1988 election, and he was pulling no punches. His Democratic opponent, Commonwealth of Massachusetts Governor Michael Dukakis, had, like virtually every state governor across the nation (including Ronald Reagan), furloughed prisoners who had later committed crimes.

Crime was a big issue in the 80s. Major cities waged war on violence, and many, especially New York City, were successful. Fear and anger, however, remained ripe for political picking. The revolving door ad became known as the "Willie Horton" ad, although Horton, who was well known at the time, is never specifically mentioned. Horton had been convicted for murder before being furloughed, and, once out, committed rape and armed robbery. The Bush-Quayle campaign used Horton's infamy as a tool to portray Dukakis as soft on crime. The ad may have contributed to Dukakis' defeat, but was later criticized as veiled racism since it obliquely referred to an African-American convict. Campaign ads are rarely even-handed and fair. It was no mistake, therefore, that this one never mentioned a certain fact: the furlough program under which Horton was released had become law before Dukakis's inauguration, during a previous Republican administration.

If omitting pertinent facts is lying, do all campaign commercials lie? Probably. At least the vast majority do. It is also perhaps fair to say that campaign ads, however entertaining they may be, are among the least reliable sources of information you will find on the internet or TV. The problem is not so much that they are misleading but that they are so effective. Campaigns and interest groups spend hundreds of millions of dollars on them because they work.

The fact that campaign ads create effective illusions supports history's most consistent complaint about democracy: people are ignorant, malleable, and vulnerable, and are therefore incapable of governing themselves. Socrates made this point some 2,400 years ago. In Plato's *Republic*, Socrates compares citizens in a democracy to troglodytes (cave dwellers) whose thoughts are manipulated by their fascination with images cast upon a wall. The images are created by democratic politicians who dangle marionettes in front of a fire. All this manipulative activity is hidden from the view of the citizens, who are chained to a wall below. We would do well to heed Socrates' warning and examine the images dangled before us, and that is what this assignment is all about.

The instructions may require a bit of research, but they are quite simple.

First, find an interesting political ad. You will find them all over the Internet, and many are on YouTube. An especially good place to start is www.livingroom-candidate.org, which presents the most prominent ads in presidential campaigns from the present all the way back to the early 1950s.

Second, write an essay (perhaps five pages long, but ask your instructor about the length) in which, in a series of clear, concise, and well-written paragraphs, you complete the following tasks. You will find the information you want in the many news and political sites on the Internet.

1. **Provide the political background for the ad.** Briefly describe or explain each of the following:
   - In which election year and in which race was the ad presented?
   - Who were the contestants?
   - What were the key issues in the race?
   - What groups provided the strongest support for each contestant?

2. **Describe the content of the ad.** Describe the images presented in it. Write a transcript of the verbal content like the one above for the revolving door ad.

3. **Identify the message.** What, exactly, is this ad trying to say?

4. **Identify the goal of the ad.** Now, in one sense, all campaign ads are aimed at getting someone elected, but be more specific. Ads are always aimed at getting someone to vote, but most are aimed at some people in particular. Who is the audience for this ad? Wealthy suburbanites? Latinos? Men? Women? Older voters? Environmentalists? Unemployed workers?

5. **Identify the strategy.** Studies show that people who actually make the effort to vote are more likely to vote *against* something than *for* something. If you can motivate people to vote, you can win an election. Emotions motivate. What is it about the ad you select that *motivates* people to vote? Fear? Hope? Jealousy? Compassion? What artistic and psychological *techniques* does it use to generate the emotion it is after? Does the ad appeal to reason? Describe the emotional and intellectual content of the visual images. How is color used? Are the images "hard" or "soft," slow or rapid, cartoonish or sophisticated? Describe the emotional and intellectual content of the words spoken. Does it connect a particular candidate with popular symbols? With negative symbols? Was the ad largely positive (portraying the good qualities of a favored candidate) or negative (portraying a candidate's weaknesses)? Some commentators claim that all political ads are negative because even seemingly positive ones inherently portray the opposing candidate as inferior in comparison.

6. **Evaluate the ad.** What has been said about it on blogs or in editorials or other political commentary? What is your personal impression of the ad? In your opinion, how effective was it in achieving its goal?

7.2   Analyze a Local Government Policy

Ariel Kaminer is a contributor to the *New York Times* who calls himself the "City Critic." Like other New Yorkers, he is sometimes frustrated by the Big Apple's crowds and how difficult it is to get around the city. In the June 4, 2010, edition of the *Times* online, Kaminer did a bit of policy analysis. Noting that the streets and subways are over-crowed but the Hudson River is relatively unused, Kaminer examined the city's system of water taxis. He found that if the city provided more piers and some coordination, water taxis could be taking thousands more New Yorkers to their daily destinations. That's what policy analysis is, finding out what a government is or is not doing and discovering a way to do things better. Just like Ariel Kaminer, you may come up with a good idea for your hometown.

A *policy* is a solution to a problem. Every day governments at all levels encounter new problems and then formulate policies in order to solve them. Policies may result in many different actions being taken, such as laws being passed or new programs being established. A small city, for example, may find that its population growth has placed new demands on its water supply. A city that needs more water might establish a policy to restrict certain types of water usage or build a new reservoir or institute new water conservation measures. Most policies are periodically reviewed and evaluated and altered to meet changing conditions. These reviews and evaluations are called *policy analyses*.

In this assignment you will be analyzing a specific, current policy of a specific local (city, town, or county) government. A local government policy analysis is advice. It is a document written to provide a decision-maker with guidance on how to create or revise a specific policy so that community needs may be better served. You will write your local government policy analysis by taking five steps:

1. Identify a specific local government policy.
2. Identify the problem(s) the policy was created to solve.
3. Evaluate the effectiveness and efficiency of the policy.
4. Identify different alternative ways to solve the problem.
5. Identify ways in which the policy could be improved and make a recommendation.

1. Identify a specific local government policy. Perhaps the most useful way to select a topic for a local government policy analysis is to tie your search to your own interests, perhaps one that relates to your future vocation. You may find a topic by asking yourself: "What are my career goals, and in what ways will government affect my ability to achieve them? Local governments affect all of our lives by providing transportation, health, safety, and other services. If you want to be a teacher, you may want to investigate current problems in a local school, like lack of funding for textbooks or the lack of physical education programs. If you are an aspiring athlete, you may want to inquire about opportunities for developing your skills in your community. Are there enough soccer fields? Bicycle paths? If medical school is in your future, you may want to investigate accessibility to emergency medical services in your neighborhood. Every day your local newspaper, in print and online, contains viable topics for local government policy analysis, and Sunday editions usually discuss a variety of issues in detail. Sometimes newspapers will highlight community problems and activities on a specific day of the week.

Remember that local government policy analysis topics should have an appropriate scope. A common mistake is for students to choose topics that are too complex or that require special technical knowledge or skills beyond those readily available. Investigating parent/faculty conflict at your local high school, for example, could be interesting and accomplishable, while checking on the town's water quality standards might make you wish you had been a chemistry major.

Once you have decided on a general topic of personal interest, an excellent way to narrow the topic is to contact a public administrator concerned with that subject and have that person identify a related problem currently facing his or her agency. Someone in your city planning office, for example, could tell you about plans for future parks and recreation facilities. At the police department you may find a public relations officer who will tell you about crime rates and what his or her department is doing to keep the community safe.

2. Identify the problem(s) the policy was created to solve. You will usually find it essential to interview public officials, representatives of interest groups, and/or technical experts to get all the information necessary to write a local government policy analysis. Information from news stories may help get you started on a topic, but they rarely have enough accurate information for a good analysis. As just mentioned, you will probably find that a local government official will be very helpful. Your local government Web site will identify people to call and their contact information. Call and make an appointment.

During your appointment you will want to ask the public official to provide you with

- General background information on the topic you have chosen
- A written copy of whatever policies may be in effect with respect to the topic
- An explanation about why particular policies were adopted, especially precisely what problem they were meant to solve
- A copy of any studies that have been conducted on the problem or the policies in place
- Information about other people and agencies who can provide you with more information

Once you have this information, identify a specific problem and a specific policy that has been created to solve that problem.

3. Evaluate the effectiveness and efficiency of the policy. From the information provided during interview(s) and from your other sources of information, attempt to assess the policy. First, you will want to come to some conclusions about how *effective* the policy is. In other words, how well does the policy you have selected actually solve the problem it was intended to solve? If a city has created a program to encourage neighborhood watch plans for suburban neighborhoods, for example, has this program had any effect on crime rates in the area?

Second, attempt to estimate the *efficiency* of the policy. Efficiency is the relationship of a program's effectiveness to its cost. For example, if a city spent $10,000 to create a network of neighborhood watch programs, and crime in those neighborhoods was reduced by 50 percent, saving the involved suburbanites $500,000, then the program could be said to be highly efficient.

4. Identify different alternative ways to solve the problem. If the policy has not completely resolved the problem at which it was aimed, are there other ways to solve the problem? You may want to do some online research to see what other cities and towns have done, to determine whether someone in another locality has a better idea.

5. Identify ways in which the policy could be improved and make a recommendation. By the time you have come this far you should be able to make a recommendation to the people responsible for creating or implementing the policy. Perhaps they should continue with the current policy exactly as it is. Perhaps a change in policy would be beneficial. In any case, be very clear and specific and state precisely what you believe ought to be done.

CHAPTER 8

Write to Explain and Evaluate Others' Work

8.1   Review a Book

Successful book reviews answer three questions:

- What did the writer of the book try to communicate?
- How clearly and convincingly did he or she get this message across to the reader?
- Was the message worth reading?

Capable book reviewers of several centuries have answered these three questions well. People who read a book review want to know if a particular book is worth reading, for their own particular purposes, before buying or reading it. These potential readers want to know the book's subject and its strengths and weaknesses, and they want to gain this information as easily and quickly as possible. Your goal in writing a book review, therefore, is to help people efficiently decide whether to buy or read a book. Your immediate objectives may be to please your instructor and get a good grade, but these objectives are most likely to be met if you focus on a book review's audience: people who want help in selecting books to buy or read. In the process of writing a book review that reaches this primary goal, you will also:

- Learn about the book you are reviewing
- Learn about professional standards for book reviews in political science
- Learn the essential steps of book reviewing that apply to any academic discipline

This final objective, learning to review a book properly, has more applications than you may at first imagine. First, it helps you to focus quickly on the essential elements of a book, and to draw from a book its informational value for yourself and others. Some of the most successful people in government, business, and the professions speed-read several books a week, more for the knowledge they contain than for enjoyment. These readers then apply this knowledge to substantial advantage in their professions. It is normally not wise to speed-read a book you are reviewing because you are unlikely to gain enough information to evaluate it fairly from such a fast reading. Writing book reviews, however, helps you become proficient in quickly sorting out valuable information from material that is not. The ability to make such discriminations is a fundamental ingredient in management and professional success.

In addition, writing book reviews for publication allows you to participate in the discussions of the broader intellectual and professional community of which you are a part. People in law, medicine, teaching, engineering, administration, and other fields are frequently asked to write book reviews to help others assess newly released publications.

Before beginning your book review, read the following sample. It is Gregory M. Scott's review of *Political Islam: Revolution, Radicalism, or Reform?*, edited by John L. Esposito. The review appeared in volume 26 of the *Southeastern Political Science Review* (June 1998) and is reprinted here by permission:

Behold an epitaph for the specter of monolithically autocratic Islam. In its survey of Islamic political movements from Pakistan to Algeria, *Political Islam: Revolution, Radicalism, or Reform?* effectively lays to rest the popular notion that political expressions of Islam are inherently violent and authoritarian. For this accomplishment alone John L. Esposito and company's scholarly anthology merits the attention of serious students of religion and politics, and justifies the book's own claim to making a "seminal contribution." Although it fails to identify how Islam as religious faith and cultural tradition lends Muslim politics a distinctively Islamic flavor, this volume clearly answers the question posed by its title: yes, political Islam encompasses not only revolution and radicalism, but moderation and reform as well.

Although two of the eleven contributors are historians, *Political Islam* exhibits both the strengths and weaknesses of contemporary political science with respect to religion. It identifies connections between economics and politics, and between culture and politics, much better than it deciphers the nuances of the relationships between politics and religious belief. After a general introduction, the first three articles explore political Islam as illegal opposition, first with a summary of major movements and then with studies of Algeria and the Gulf states. In her chapter titled "Fulfilling Prophecies: State Policy and Islamist Radicalism," Lisa Anderson sets a methodological guideline for the entire volume when she writes:

Rather than look to the substance of Islam or the content of putatively Islamic political doctrines for a willingness to embrace violent means to desired ends, we might explore a different perspective and examine the political circumstances, or institutional environment, that breeds political radicalism, extremism, or violence independent of the content of the doctrine (18).

Therefore, rather than assessing how Islam as religion affects Muslim politics, all the subsequent chapters proceed to examine politics, economics, and culture in a variety of Muslim nations. This means that the title of the book is slightly misleading: it discusses Muslim politics rather than political Islam. Esposito provides the book's conclusion about the effects of Islamic belief on the political process when he maintains that "the appeal to religion is a two-edged sword. . . . It can provide or enhance self-legitimation, but it can also be used as a yardstick for judgment by opposition forces and delegitimation" (70).

The second part of the volume features analyses of the varieties of political processes in Iran, Sudan, Egypt, and Pakistan. These chapters clearly demonstrate not only that Islamic groups may be found in varied positions on normal economic and ideological spectrums, but that Islam is not necessarily opposed to moderate, pluralist politics. The third section of the anthology examines the international relations of Hamas, Afghani Islamists, and Islamic groups involved in the Middle East peace process. These chapters are especially important for American students because they present impressive documentation for the conclusions that the motives and demands of many Islamic groups are considerably more moderate and reasonable than much Western political commentary would suggest.

The volume is essentially well written. All the articles with the exception of chapter two avoid unnecessarily dense political science jargon. As a collection of methodologically sound and analytically astute treatments of Muslim politics, *Political Islam: Revolution, Radicalism, or Reform?* is certainly appropriate for adoption as a supplemental text for courses in religion and politics. By way of noting what it does not cover, readers may consider that although it is sufficient for its purposes as it stands, the volume could be a primary text in a course on Islamic politics if it included four additional chapters:

1. An historical overview of the origins and varieties of Islam as religion
2. A summary of the global Islamic political–ideological spectrum (from liberal to fundamentalist)
3. An overview of the varieties of global Islamic cultures
4. An attempt to describe in what manner, if any, Islam, in all its varieties, gives politics a different flavor from the politics of other major religions

Elements of a Book Review

Book reviews in political science contain the same essential elements of all book reviews. Because political science is nonfiction, book reviews within the discipline focus less on a work's writing style and more on its content and method than do reviews of fiction. Your book review should generally contain four basic elements, although not always in this order:

1. Enticement
2. Examination
3. Elucidation
4. Evaluation

Enticement. Your first sentence should entice people to read your review. A crisp summary of what the book is about entices your readers because it lets them know that you can quickly and clearly come to the point. They know that their time and efforts will not be wasted in an attempt to wade through your vague prose in hopes of finding out something about the book. Notice Scott's opening line: "Behold an epitaph for the specter of monolithically autocratic Islam." It is a bit overburdened with large words, but it is engaging and precisely sums up the essence of the review. Your opening statement can be engaging and "catchy," but be sure that it provides an accurate portrayal of the book in one crisp statement.

Examination. Your book review should allow the reader to join you in examining the book. Tell the reader what the book is about. One of the greatest strengths of Scott's review is that his first paragraph immediately tells you exactly what he thinks the book accomplishes.

When you review a book, write about what is actually in the book, not what you think is probably there or ought to be there. Do not explain how you would have written the book, but instead how the author wrote it. Describe the book in clear, objective terms. Tell enough about the content to identify the author's major points.

Elucidation. Elucidate, or clarify, the book's value and contribution to political science by defining (1) what the author is attempting to do and (2) how the author's work fits within current similar efforts in the discipline of political science or scholarly inquiry in general. Notice how Scott immediately describes what Esposito is trying to do: "This volume clearly answers the question posed by its title." Scott precedes this definition of the author's purpose by placing his work within the context of current similar writing in political science by stating that "for this accomplishment alone John L. Esposito and company's scholarly anthology merits the attention of serious students of religion and politics, and justifies the book's own claim to making a 'seminal contribution.'"

The elucidation portion of book reviews often provides additional information about the author. Scott has not included such information about Esposito in his review, but it would be helpful to know, for example, if Esposito has written other books on the subject, has developed a reputation for exceptional expertise on a certain issue, or is known to have a particular ideological bias. How would your understanding of this book be changed, for example, if you knew that its author were a leader of Hamas or the PLO? Include information in your book review about the author that helps the reader understand how this book fits within the broader concerns of political science.

Evaluation.   Once you explain what the book is attempting to do, you should tell the reader the extent to which this goal has been met. To evaluate a book effectively, you will need to establish evaluation criteria and then compare the book's content to those criteria. You do not need to define your criteria specifically in your review, but they should be evident to the reader. Your criteria will vary according to the book you are reviewing, and you may discuss them in any order that is helpful to the reader. Consider, however, including the following among the criteria that you establish for your book review:

- How important is the subject to the study of politics and government?
- How complete and thorough is the author's coverage of the subject?
- How carefully is the author's analysis conducted?
- What are the strengths and limitations of the author's methodology?
- What is the quality of the writing? Is it clear, precise, and interesting?
- How does this book compare with others on the subject?
- What contribution does this book make to political science?
- Who will enjoy or benefit from this book?

When giving your evaluations according to these criteria, be specific. If you write, "This is a good book; I liked it very much," you tell nothing of interest or value to the reader. Notice, however, how Scott's review helps to clearly define the content and the limitations of the book by contrasting the volume with what he describes as an ideal primary text for a course in Islamic politics: "By way of noting what it does not cover, readers may consider that although it is sufficient for its purposes as it stands, the volume could be a primary text in a course on Islamic politics if it included four additional chapters."

Qualities of Effective Political Science Book Reviews
Effective political science book reviews

- Serve the reader
- Are fair
- Are concise and specific, not vague and general

Write your review with the potential reader, not yourself or the book's author, in mind. The person who may read the book is, in a manner of speaking, your client.

Your reader wants a fair review of the book. Do not be overly generous to a book of poor quality, but do not be too critical of an honest effort to tackle a very complex or difficult problem. If you have a bias that may affect your review, let your reader know this, but do so briefly. Do not shift the focus from the book's ideas to your own. Do not attack a work because of the author's politics. Do not chide the author for not having written a book different from the one he or she has written.

The reader of your book review is not interested in your thoughts about politics or other subjects. Try to appreciate the author's efforts and goals, and sympathize with the author, but remain sufficiently detached to identify errors. Try to show the book's strengths and weaknesses as clearly as possible.

Write a review that is interesting, appealing, and even charming, but not at the expense of accuracy or of the book being reviewed. Be erudite but not prolix. (To be *erudite* is to display extensive knowledge. To be *prolix* is to be wordy and vague.) Your goal is to display substantial knowledge of the book's content, strengths, and weaknesses in as few words as possible.

Preliminaries: Before Writing a Book Review
Before sitting down to write your review, make sure you do the following:

- **Get further directions from your instructor.** Ask if there are specific directions beyond those in this manual for the number of pages or the content of the review.
- **Read the book.** Reviewers who skim or merely read a book's jacket do a great disservice to the author. Read the book thoroughly.
- **Respond to the book.** As you read, make notes on your responses to the book. Organize them into the categories of enticement, examination, elucidation, and evaluation.
- **Get to know the subject.** Use your library to find a summary of works on the issue. Such a summary may be found in a review, in a journal, or in a recent textbook on the subject.
- **Familiarize yourself with other books by the author.** If the author has written other works, learn enough about them to be able to describe them briefly to your readers.
- **Read reviews of other political science books.** Many political science journals have book review sections, usually at the end of an issue. Go to the library and browse through some of the reviews in several journals. Not only will you get to know what is expected from a political science book review, but you will also find many interesting ideas on how books are approached and evaluated.

Format and Content
The directions for writing papers provided in Chapters 1 through 4 apply to book reviews as well. Some further instructions specific to book reviews are needed, however. First, list on the title page, along with the standard information required for political science papers, data on the book being reviewed: title, author, place and

name of publisher, date, and number of pages. As the sample that follows shows, the title of the book should be in italics or underlined, but not both:

Reflective or Analytical Book Reviews

Instructors in the humanities and social sciences normally assign two types of book reviews: the *reflective* and the *analytical*. Ask your instructor which type of book review you are to write. The purpose of a reflective book review is for the student reviewer to exercise creative analytical judgment without being influenced by the reviews of others. Reflective book reviews contain all the elements covered in this chapter—enticement, examination, elucidation, and evaluation—but they do not include the views of others who have also read the book.

Analytical book reviews contain all the information provided by reflective reviews but add an analysis of the comments of other reviewers. The purpose is, thus, to review not only the book itself but also its reception in the professional community.

To write an analytical book review, insert a review analysis section immediately after your summary of the book. To prepare this section, use the *Book Review Digest* and *Book Review Index* in the library to locate other reviews of the book that have been published in journals and other periodicals. As you read these reviews:

1. List the criticisms of the book's strengths and weaknesses that are made in the reviews.
2. Develop a concise summary of these criticisms, indicate the overall positive or negative tone of the reviews, and mention some of the most commonly found comments.
3. Evaluate the criticisms found in these reviews. Are they basically accurate in their assessment of the book?
4. Write a review analysis of two pages or less that states and evaluates steps 2 and 3 above, and place it in your book review immediately after your summary of the book.

Length of a Book Review

Unless your instructor gives you other directions, a reflective book review should be three to five typed pages long, and an analytical book review should be five to seven pages long. In either case, a brief, specific, and concise book review is almost always preferred over one of greater length.

8.2   Critique an Article

An *article critique* is a paper that evaluates an article published in an academic journal. A good critique tells the reader what point the article is trying to make and how convincingly it makes that point. Writing an article critique achieves three purposes. First, it provides you with an understanding of the information contained in a scholarly article and a familiarity with other information written on the same topic. Second, it provides you with an opportunity to apply and develop your critical thinking skills as you attempt to critically evaluate a political scientist's work. Third, it helps you to improve your own writing skills as you attempt to describe the selected article's strengths and weaknesses so that your readers can clearly understand them.

The first step in writing an article critique is to select an appropriate article. Unless your instructor specifies otherwise, select an article from a scholarly journal (such as the *American Political Science Review, Journal of Politics*, or *Southeastern Political Science Review*) and not a popular or journalistic publication (such as *Time* or the *National Review*). Appendix A of this manual includes a substantial list of academic political science journals, but your instructor may also accept appropriate articles from academic journals in other disciplines, such as history, economics, or sociology.

Choosing an Article

Three other considerations should guide your choice of an article. First, browse article titles until you find a topic that interests you. Writing a critique will be much more satisfying if you have an interest in the topic. Hundreds of interesting journal articles are published every year. The second consideration in selecting an article is your current level of knowledge. Many political science studies, for example, employ sophisticated statistical techniques. You may be better prepared to evaluate them if you have studied statistics.

The third consideration is to select a current article, one written within the last twelve months. Most material in political science is quickly superseded by new studies. Selecting a recent study will help ensure that you will be engaged in an up-to-date discussion of your topic.

Writing the Critique

Once you have selected and carefully read your article, you may begin to write your critique, which will cover five areas:

1. Thesis
2. Methods
3. Evidence of thesis support
4. Contribution to the literature
5. Recommendation

Thesis.   Your first task is to find and clearly state the thesis of the article. The thesis is the main point the article is trying to make. In a 1997 article entitled "Unequal Participation: Democracy's Unresolved Dilemma," APSA President Arend Lijphart, Research Professor of Political Science at the University of California, San Diego, states his thesis very clearly:

> Low voter turnout is a serious democratic problem for five reasons: (1) It means unequal turnout that is systematically biased against less well-to-do citizens. (2) Unequal turnout spells unequal political influence. (3) U.S. voter turnout is especially low, but, measured as percent of voting-age population, it is also relatively low in most other countries. (4) Turnout in midterm, regional, local, and supranational elections—less salient but by no means unimportant elections—tends to be especially poor. (5) Turnout appears to be declining everywhere.

Many authors, however, do not present their theses this clearly. After you have read the article, ask yourself whether you had to hunt for the thesis. Comment about the clarity of the author's thesis presentation and state the author's thesis in your critique. Before proceeding with the remaining elements of your critique, consider the importance of the topic. Has the author written something that is important for us as citizens or political scientists to read?

Methods.   In your critique, carefully answer the following questions:

1. What methods did the author use to investigate the topic? In other words, how did the author go about supporting the thesis?
2. Were the appropriate methods used?
3. Did the author's approach to supporting the thesis make sense?
4. Did the author employ the selected methods correctly?
5. Did you discover any errors in the way he or she conducted the research?

Evidence of Thesis Support

In your critique, answer the following questions:

1. What evidence did the author present in support of the thesis?
2. What are the strengths of the evidence presented?
3. What are the weaknesses of the evidence?
4. On balance, how well did the author support the thesis?

Contribution to the Literature.   This step will probably require you to undertake some research of your own. Identify articles and books published within the past five years on the subject of your selected article. Browse the titles and read perhaps half a dozen of the publications that appear to provide the best discussion of the topic. In your critique, list the most important other articles or books that have been published on your topic and then, in view of these publications, evaluate the contribution that your selected article makes to a better understanding of the subject.

Recommendation.   In this section of your critique, summarize your evaluation of the article. Tell your readers several things: Who will benefit from reading this article? What will the benefit be? How important and extensive is that benefit? Clearly state your evaluation of the article in the form of a thesis for your own critique. Your thesis might be something like the following:

> Arend Lijphart's article entitled "Unequal Participation: Democracy's Unresolved Dilemma" is the most concise and comprehensive discussion of the problem of unequal participation published in recent years. Political scientists should conscientiously confront Lijphart's warning because he conclusively demonstrates that unequal participation presents an imminent threat to American democracy.

When writing this assignment, follow the directions for paper formats in Chapter 4 of this manual. Ask your instructor for directions concerning the length of the critique, but in the absence of further guidelines, your paper should not exceed five typed, double-spaced pages.

Part III
Move Forward: Conduct Research in Political Science

CHAPTER 9
Organize the Research Process

9.1   Establish an Effective Research Process

The research paper is where all your skills as an interpreter of details, an organizer of facts and theories, and a writer of clear prose come together. Building logical arguments on the twin bases of fact and hypothesis is the way things are done in political science, and the most successful political scientists are those who master the art of research.

Students new to the writing of research papers sometimes find themselves intimidated by the job ahead of them. After all, the research paper adds what seems to be an extra set of complexities to the writing process. As any other expository or persuasive paper does, a research paper must present an original thesis using a carefully organized and logical argument. But it also investigates a topic that is outside the writer's own experience. This means that writers must locate and evaluate information that is new, thus, in effect, educating themselves as they explore their topics. A beginning researcher sometimes feels overwhelmed by the basic requirements of the assignment or by the authority of the source material being investigated.

As you begin a research project, it may be difficult to establish a sense of control over the different tasks you are undertaking. You may have little notion of where to search for a thesis or even for the most helpful information. If you do not carefully monitor your own work habits, you may find yourself unwittingly abdicating responsibility for the paper's argument by borrowing it wholesale from one or more of your sources.

Who is in control of your paper? The answer must be you—not the instructor who assigned the paper to you, and certainly not the published writers and interviewees whose opinions you solicit. If all your paper does is paste together the opinions of others, it has little use. It is up to you to synthesize an original idea from a judicious evaluation of your source material. At the beginning of your research project, you will, of course, be unsure about many elements of your paper. For example, you will probably not yet have a definitive thesis sentence or even much understanding of the shape of your argument. But you can establish a measure of control over the process you will go through to complete the paper. And, if you work regularly and systematically, keeping yourself open to new ideas as they present themselves, your sense of control will grow. Here are some suggestions to help you establish and maintain control of your paper:

1. **Understand your assignment.** It is possible for a research assignment to go badly simply because the writer did not read the assignment carefully. Considering how

much time and effort you are about to put into your project, it is a very good idea to make sure you have a clear understanding of what your instructor wants you to do. Be sure to ask your instructor about any aspect of the assignment that is unclear to you—but only after you have read it carefully. Recopying the assignment in your own handwriting is a good way to start, even though your instructor may have already given it to you in writing. Before you dive into the project, make sure that you have considered the questions listed below.

2. **What is your topic?** The assignment may give you a great deal of specific information about your topic, or you may be allowed considerable freedom in establishing one for yourself. In a government class in which you are studying issues affecting American foreign policy, your professor might give you a very specific assignment—a paper, for example, examining the difficulties of establishing a viable foreign policy in the wake of the collapse of international communism—or he or she may allow you to choose for yourself the issue that your paper will address. You need to understand the terms, as set up in the assignment, by which you will design your project.

3. **What is your purpose?** Whatever the degree of latitude you are given in the matter of your topic, pay close attention to the way your instructor has phrased the assignment. Is your primary job to *describe* a current political situation or to *take a stand* on it? Are you to *compare* political systems, and if so, to what end? Are you to *classify, persuade, survey,* or *analyze*? To determine the purpose of the project, look for such descriptive terms in the assignment.

4. **Who is your audience?** Your own orientation to the paper is profoundly affected by your conception of the audience for whom you are writing. Granted that your main reader is your instructor, who else would be interested in your paper? Are you writing for the voters of a community, a governor, or a city council? A paper that describes the proposed renovation of city buildings may justifiably contain much more technical jargon for an audience of contractors than for a council of local business and civic leaders.

5. **What kind of research are you doing?** You will be doing one if not both of the following kinds of research:

■ *Primary research*, which requires you to discover information firsthand, often by conducting interviews, surveys, or polls. In primary research, you are collecting and sifting through raw data—data that have not already been interpreted by researchers—which you will then study, select, arrange, and speculate on. These raw data may be the opinions of experts or of people on the street, historical documents, the published letters of a famous politician, or material collected from other researchers. It is important to set up carefully the methods by which you collect your data. Your aim is to gather the most accurate information possible, from which sound observations may be made later, either by you or by other writers using the material you have uncovered.

■ *Secondary research*, which uses published accounts of primary materials. Although the primary researcher might poll a community for its opinion on the outcome of a recent bond election, the secondary researcher will use the material from the poll to support a particular thesis. Secondary research, in other words, focuses on interpretations of raw data. Most of your college papers will be based on your use of secondary sources.

PRIMARY SOURCE	SECONDARY SOURCE
A published collection of Thurgood Marshall's letters	A journal article arguing that the volume of letters illustrates Marshall's attitude toward the media
An interview with the mayor	A character study of the mayor based on the interview
Material from a questionnaire	A paper basing its thesis on the results of the questionnaire

6. **Keep your perspective.** Whichever type of research you perform, you must keep your results in perspective. There is no way that you, as a primary researcher, can be completely objective in your findings. It is not possible to design a questionnaire that will net you absolute truth, nor can you be sure that the opinions you gather in interviews reflect the accurate and unchanging opinions of the people you question. Likewise, if you are conducting secondary research, you must remember that the articles and journals you are reading are shaped by the aims of their writers, who are interpreting primary materials for their own ends. The farther you are removed from a primary source, the greater the possibility for distortion. Your job as a researcher is to be as accurate as possible, which means keeping in view the limitations of your methods and their ends.

In any research project, there will be moments of confusion, but you can prevent this confusion from overwhelming you by establishing an effective research procedure. You need to design a schedule that is as systematic as possible, yet flexible enough so that you do not feel trapped by it. By always showing you what to do next, a schedule will help keep you from running into dead ends. At the same time, the schedule helps you retain the focus necessary to spot new ideas and new strategies as you work.

Give Yourself Plenty of Time

You may feel like delaying your research for many reasons: unfamiliarity with the library, the press of other tasks, a deadline that seems comfortably far away. But do not allow such factors to deter you. Research takes time. Working in a library seems to speed up the clock, so that the hour you expected it would take you to find a certain source becomes two. You must allow yourself the time needed not only to find material but also to read it, assimilate it, and set it in the context of your own thoughts. If you delay starting, you may well find yourself distracted by the deadline, having to keep an eye on the clock while trying to make sense of a writer's complicated argument.

The following schedule lists the steps of a research project in the order in which they are generally accomplished. Remember that each step is dependent on the others and that it is quite possible to revise earlier decisions in light of later discoveries. After some background reading, for example, your notion of the paper's purpose may change, a fact that may in turn alter other steps. One of the strengths of a good schedule is its flexibility. Note that this schedule lists tasks for both primary and secondary research; you should use only those steps that are relevant to your project.

9.2   Find and Evaluate the Quality of Online and Printed Information

Do Background Reading

Whether you are doing primary or secondary research, you need to know what kinds of work have already been done in your field. **WARNING:** Be very careful not to rely too heavily on material in general encyclopedias such as *Wikipedia* or *Encyclopaedia Britannica*. You may wish to consult one for an overview of a topic with which you are unfamiliar, but students new to research are often tempted to import large sections, if not entire articles, from such volumes, and this practice is not good scholarship. One major reason your instructor has assigned a research paper is to let you experience the kinds of books and journals in which the discourse of political science is conducted. Encyclopedias are good places for instant introductions to subjects; some even include bibliographies of reference works at the ends of their articles. But to write a useful paper, you will need much more detailed information about your subject. Once you have learned what you can from a general encyclopedia, move on to the academic articles that you will find by following links on your college library's Web page. When you find two or three good articles on your topic, you will find that the bibliographies at the end of each article will be rich sources of other articles and books of academically acceptable quality.

Narrow Your Topic and Establish a Working Thesis

The process of coming up with a viable thesis for a paper involving academic research is pretty much the same one to use for a paper that doesn't require formal research, though the need to consult published sources may seem to make the enterprise more intimidating. (Chapter 1 offers general tips for finding a successful thesis for a paper.) For a research paper in a course in American government, Charlotte Goble was given the topic category of grassroots attempts to legislate morality in American society. She chose the specific topic of textbook censorship. Here is the path she took as she looked for ways to limit the topic effectively and find a thesis.

GENERAL TOPIC	Textbook censorship
POTENTIAL TOPICS	How a local censorship campaign gets started
	Funding censorship campaigns
	Reasons behind textbook censorship
	Results of censorship campaigns
WORKING THESIS	It is disconcertingly easy in our part of the state to launch a textbook censorship campaign

As with any paper, it is unlikely that you will come up with a satisfactory thesis at the beginning of your research project. You need a way to guide yourself through the early stages of research as you work toward discovering a main idea that is both useful and manageable. Having in mind a *working thesis*—a preliminary statement of your purpose—can help you select the material that is of greatest interest to you as you examine potential sources. The working thesis will probably evolve as your research progresses, and you should be ready to accept such change. You must not fix on a thesis too early in the process, or you may miss opportunities to refine it.

9.3   Develop a Working Bibliography

As you begin your research, you will look for published sources—essays, books, or interviews with experts—that may help you. This list of potentially useful sources is your *working bibliography*. There are many ways to develop this bibliography. The cataloging system in your library will give you sources, as will the published bibliographies in your field. (Some of these bibliographies are listed below.) The general references in which you did your background reading may also list such works, and each specialized book or essay you find will have a bibliography that its writer used, which may be helpful to you.

It is from your working bibliography that you will select the items for the bibliography that will appear in the final draft of your paper. Early in your research, you will not know which of the sources will help you and which will not, but it is important to keep an accurate description of each entry in your working bibliography so that you will be able to tell clearly which items you have investigated and which you will need to consult again. Establishing the working bibliography also allows you to practice using the bibliographical format you are required to follow in your final draft. As you make your list of potential sources, be sure to include all the information about each one, in the proper format, using the proper punctuation. (Chapter 4 describes in detail the bibliographical formats most often required for political science papers.)

Write for Needed Information

In the course of your research, you may need to consult a source that is not immediately available to you. Working on a textbook censorship paper, for example, you might find that a packet of potentially useful information may be obtained from a government agency or public interest group in Washington, DC. Or you may discover that a needed book is not owned by your university library or by any other local library, or that a successful antidrug program has been implemented in the school system of a city of comparable size in another state. In such situations, it may be tempting to disregard potential sources because of the difficulty of consulting them. If you ignore this material, however, you are not doing your job.

It is vital that you take steps to acquire the needed data. In the first case mentioned above, you can simply write to the Washington, DC, agency or interest group; in the second, you may use your library's interlibrary loan procedure to obtain the book; in the third, you can track down the council that manages the antidrug campaign by e-mail, phone, or Internet, and ask for information. Remember that many businesses and government agencies want to share their information with interested citizens; some have employees or entire departments whose job is to facilitate communication with the public. Be as specific as possible when asking for such information. It is a good idea to outline your own project briefly—in no more than a few sentences—to help the respondent determine the types of information that will be useful to you.

Never let the immediate unavailability of a source stop you from trying to consult it. And be sure to begin the job of locating and acquiring such long-distance material as soon as possible, to allow for the various delays that often occur.

Evaluate Written Sources

Fewer research experiences are more frustrating than trying to recall information found in a source that you can no longer identify. You must establish an efficient method of examining and evaluating the sources in your working bibliography. Suggestions for compiling an accurate record of your written sources are described below.

Determine Quickly the Potential Usefulness of a Source

For books, you can read the front material (the introduction, foreword, and preface), looking for the author's thesis; you can also examine chapter headings, dust jackets, and indexes. A journal article should announce its intention in its introduction, which in most cases will be a page or less in length. This sort of preliminary examination should tell you whether a more intensive examination is worthwhile. Whatever you decide about the source, copy its title page, making sure to include all important publication information (including title, date, author, volume number, and page numbers). Without such a record, later in your research, you might forget that you have consulted a particular text and find yourself repeating your work.

When you have determined that a potential source is worth closer inspection, explore it carefully. If it is a book, determine whether you should invest the time needed to read it in its entirety. Whatever the source, make sure you understand not only its overall thesis but also each part of the argument that the writer sets up to illustrate or prove the thesis. You need to get a feel for the writer's argument—how the subtopics form (or do not form) a logical defense of the main point. What do you think of the writer's logic and the examples used? You may need more than one reading to arrive at an accurate appraisal.

Important: *Own* Your Source Material

As you conduct your research in the age of the Internet, it's easy simply to slide information that catches your attention from one machine, one medium, one database, to another without changing a word of it. But cutting a paragraph or phrase out of an online essay to place in a file of source material, while convenient, also hides a danger to watch out for: the danger that you won't really assimilate the material in the excerpt—its facts, its argument, its tone—as completely as necessary to make the most effective use of it. Nothing prompts you to *own* research material, to understand it clearly and with confidence, quite like rephrasing it in your own words. Remember the point made on the first page of Chapter 1 of this manual: Writing is one of the best ways to learn. For this reason, whether you collect research information using a computer keyboard or using the old-fashioned method of scribbling quick notes on cards, it's an extremely good idea to put the material in your own words—making sure, of course, that you do justice to the author's point.

As you read, try to get a feel for the larger argument in which the source takes its place. Its references to the works of other writers will show you where to look for additional material and indicate the general shape of scholarly opinion concerning your subject. If you can see the source you are reading as only one element of an ongoing dialogue, instead of the last word on the subject, then you can place its argument in perspective.

Determine Whether Interviews or Surveys Are Needed

If your project calls for primary research, you may need to use a questionnaire to interview experts on your topic or to conduct a survey of opinions among a select group. Be sure to prepare yourself as thoroughly as possible for any primary research. Here are some tips.

Conducting an Interview.   Establish a purpose for each interview, bearing in mind the requirements of your working thesis. In what ways might your interview benefit your paper? Write down your description of the interview's purpose. Estimate its length, and inform your subject. Arrive for your interview on time and dressed appropriately. Be courteous.

Before the interview, learn as much as possible about your topic by researching published sources. Use this research to design your questions. If possible, learn something about the backgrounds of the people you interview. This knowledge may help you establish rapport with your subjects and will also help you tailor your questions. Take with you to the interview a list of prepared questions. However, be ready during the interview to depart from your list in order to follow any potentially useful direction that the questioning may take.

Take notes. Make sure you have extra pens. Do not use a tape recorder because it will inhibit most interviewees. If you must use tape, *ask for permission from your subject* before beginning the interview. Follow up your interview with a thank-you letter and, if feasible, a copy of the paper in which the interview is used.

Designing and Conducting a Survey. If your research requires a survey, see Chapter 10 for instructions on designing and conducting surveys, polls, and questionnaires.

9.4 Conduct a Formal Literature Review

Your goal in writing a research paper is to provide an opportunity for your readers to increase their understanding of the subject you are addressing. They will want the most current and precise information available. Whether you are writing a traditional library research paper, conducting an experiment, or preparing an analysis of a policy enforced by a government agency, you must know what has already been learned in order to give your readers comprehensive and up-to-date information or to add something new to what they already know about the subject. If your topic is welfare administration in Tennessee, for example, you will want to find out precisely what national, state, and local government policies currently affect welfare administration in Tennessee, and the important details of how and why these policies came to be adopted. When you seek this information, you will be conducting a *literature review*, a thoughtful collection and analysis of available information on the topic you have selected for study. It tells you, before you begin your paper, experiment, or analysis, what is already known about the subject.

Why do you need to conduct a literature review? It would be embarrassing to spend a lot of time and effort preparing a study, only to find that the information you are seeking has already been discovered by someone else. Also, a properly conducted literature review will tell you many things about a particular subject. It will tell you the extent of current knowledge, sources of data for your research, examples of what is *not* known (which in turn generate ideas for formulating hypotheses), methods that have been previously used for research, and clear definitions of concepts relevant to your own research.

Let us consider an example. Suppose that you have decided to research the following question: "How are voter attitudes affected by negative advertising?" First, you will need to establish a clear definition of "negative advertising"; then you will need to find a way to measure attitudes of voters; finally, you will need to use or develop a method of discerning how attitudes are affected by advertising. Using research techniques explained in this and other chapters of this manual, you will begin your research by looking for studies that address your research question or similar questions in the library, on the Internet, and through other resources. You will discover that many studies have been written on voters' attitudes and the effects of advertising on them. As you read these studies, certain patterns will appear. Some research methods will seem to have produced better results than others. Some studies will be quoted in others many times—some confirming and others refuting what previous studies have done. You will constantly be making choices as you examine these studies, reading very carefully those that are highly relevant to your purposes, and skimming those that are of only marginal interest. As you read, constantly ask yourself the following questions:

- How much is known about this subject?
- What is the best available information, and why is it better than other information?
- What research methods have been used successfully in relevant studies?
- What are the possible sources of data for further investigation of this topic?
- What important information is still not known, in spite of all previous research?
- Of the methods that have been used for research, which are the most effective for making new discoveries? Are new methods needed?
- How can the concepts being researched be more precisely defined?

You will find that this process, like the research process as a whole, is recursive. Insights related to one of the above questions will spark new investigations into others, and these investigations will then bring up a new set of questions, and so on.

Your instructor may request that you include a literature review as a section of the paper that you are writing. Your written literature review may be from one to several pages in length, but it should always tell the reader the following information:

1. Which previously compiled or published studies, articles, or other documents provide the best available information on the selected topic
2. What these studies conclude about the topic
3. What the apparent methodological strengths and weaknesses of these studies are
4. What remains to be discovered about the topic
5. What appear to be, according to these studies, the most effective methods for developing new information on the topic

Your literature review should consist of a written narrative that answers—not necessarily consecutively—the above questions. The success of your own research project depends in large part on the extent to which you have carefully and thoughtfully answered these questions.

Part IV
Write for Your Political Science Course

CHAPTER 10

Analyze Public Opinion

10.1   Understand the Scope and Purpose of Your Survey

A poll is a device for counting preferences. When we go to the polls on election day, the polling officials count the preferences for candidates (and sometimes laws or other issues) that are produced when people mark their ballots. The officers then transmit these results to local, state, or national officials. A survey is a series of statements or questions that define a set of preferences to be polled. If a poll is conducted on the subject of national welfare programs, for example, a survey will be constructed consisting of a series of questions, such as "Do you think that welfare benefits ought to be increased or reduced?" or "Do you believe there is a lot of fraud in the welfare system?"

Writing your own public opinion survey paper will serve two purposes. First, you will learn how to construct, conduct, and interpret a public opinion poll, the means by which much research is done within the discipline. You will thus begin to learn a skill that you may actually use in your professional life. Large and small public and private organizations often conduct polls on the public's needs and preferences, in order to make their services more effective and desirable. Second, by writing a survey paper, you will understand how to evaluate polls thoughtfully and critically by knowing the strengths and weaknesses of the polling process.

In this chapter, you will learn how to construct and conduct a simple public opinion poll and how to apply some elementary data analysis and evaluation techniques to your poll results. Your instructor may want to add supplemental tasks, such as other statistical procedures, and your text in political science methods will tell you much more about the process of public opinion research. The following set of directions, however, will provide the information needed to create and interpret a public opinion poll.

10.2   Focus on a Specific Topic

The first step in writing a public opinion survey paper is to select a topic that is focused on one specific issue. Although nationally conducted polls sometimes cover a broad variety of topics, confining your inquiry to one narrowly defined issue will allow you to gain an appreciation for even a single topic's complexity and the difficulties inherent in clearly identifying opinions. Precision is important in clearly understanding public opinion.

Public opinion surveys are conducted on topics pertaining to local, state, national, or international politics, topics nearly as numerous as the titles of articles in a daily newspaper. You will usually increase the interest of the audience of your paper if you select an issue that is currently widely discussed in the news.

10.3   Formulate a Research Question and Hypothesis

Once you have selected a topic, your task is to determine what you want to know about people's opinions concerning that topic. If you choose the environment, for example, you may want to know the extent to which people are concerned about environmental quality. You need to phrase your questions carefully. If you ask, simply, "Are you concerned about the quality of the environment?" you will probably receive a positive reply from a substantial majority of your respondents. But what does this actually tell you? Does it reveal the depth and strength of people's concern about the environment? Do you know how the respondents will vote on any particular environmental issue? Do people have different attitudes toward air pollution, water quality, and land use? To find out, you will need to design more specific questions. The following sections of this chapter will help you to do this.

To create these specific questions, however, you will first need to formulate a research question and a research hypothesis. Before continuing, read Chapter 9 on formulating and testing research hypotheses.

A research question asks exactly what the researcher wants to know. Research questions posed by national polls include the following:

- What is the president's current approval rating?
- What types of voters are likely to favor immigration reform?
- What are the dominant current attitudes towards the national debt?

Research questions for papers for political science classes, however, should be more specific and confined to a narrowly defined topic. Consider the following:

- Is the population to be surveyed in favor of universal handgun registration legislation?
- To what extent do the people polled believe that their own personal political actions, such as voting or writing to a representative, will actually make a difference in the political process?
- What are the attitudes of the selected population toward legislation that promotes gay rights?

10.4   Select a Sample

Surveys of public opinion are usually conducted to find out what large groups of people, such as American voters, members of labor unions, or religious fundamentalists, think about a particular problem. It is normally unnecessary and too costly to obtain the views of everyone in these groups. Most surveys therefore question a small but representative percentage of the group that is being studied. The elements of surveys are the individual units being studied. Elements might be interest groups, corporations, or church denominations, but they are most often individual voters. The population is the total number of elements covered by the research question. If the research question is "Are voters in Calaveras County in favor of a 1 percent sales tax to pay for highway improvements?" then the population is the voters of Calaveras County. The sample is the part of the population that is selected to respond to the survey. A representative sample includes numbers of elements in the same proportions as they occur in the general population. In other words, if the population of Calaveras County is 14 percent Latino and 52 percent female, a representative sample will also be 14 percent Latino and 52 percent female. A nonrepresentative sample does not include numbers of elements in the same proportions as they occur in the general population.

All samples are drawn from a sampling frame, which is the part of the population being surveyed. To represent the population accurately, a sampling frame should include all types of elements (e.g., youth, women, Latinos) of interest to the research question. If the population is the voters of Calaveras County, a sampling frame might be the parents of children in an elementary school who are registered to vote. Strata are groups of similar elements within a population. Strata of the voters of Calaveras County may include voters under 30, women, labor union members, or Latinos. Stratified samples include numbers of respondents in different strata that are not in proportion to the general population. For example, a stratified sample of the population of Calaveras County might purposely include only Latino women if the purpose of the survey is to determine the views of this group.

A survey research design of the Calaveras County issue would thus be constructed as follows:

Research question: Are voters in Calaveras County in favor of a 1 percent sales tax to pay for highway improvements?

Research hypothesis: Fifty-five percent of the voters in Calaveras County will favor a 1 percent sales tax to pay for highway improvements.

Elements: Individual registered voters.

Population: Registered voters in Calaveras County.

Sampling frame: Five hundred registered voters in Calaveras County selected at random from voter registration lists.

Sample: Of the 500 registered voters in Calaveras County selected at random from voter registration lists, those who answer the survey questions when called on the telephone.

How large must a sample be in order to represent the population accurately? This question is difficult to answer, but two general principles apply. First, a large sample is more likely, simply by chance, to be more representative of a population than a small sample. Second, the goal is to obtain a sample that includes representatives of all of the strata within the whole population.

You will find it most convenient if you use as your sample the class for which you are writing your survey paper. The disadvantage of this sample selection is that your class may not be representative of the college or university in which your survey is conducted. Even if this is the case, however, you will still be learning the procedures for conducting a survey, which is the primary objective of this exercise.

■ **Note:** Public opinion surveys ask people for their opinions. The people whose opinions are sought are known as human subjects of the research. Most colleges and universities have policies concerning research with human subjects. Sometimes administrative offices known as institutional review boards are established to review research proposals in order to ensure that the rights of human subjects are protected. It may be necessary for you to obtain permission from such a board or from your college to conduct your survey. Be sure to comply with all policies of your university with respect to research with human subjects.

10.5   Construct the Survey Questionnaire

Your research question will be your primary guide for constructing your survey questions. As you begin to write your questions, ask yourself what it is that you really want to know about the topic. Suppose that your research question is, "What are the views of political science students regarding the role of the government in regulating abortions?" If you ask, for example, "Are you for abortion?" you may get a negative answer from 70 percent of the respondents. If you then ask, "Are you for making abortion illegal?" you may get a negative answer from 81 percent of your respondents. These answers seem to contradict each other. By asking additional questions you may determine that, whereas a majority of the respondents finds abortion regrettable, only a minority wants to make it illegal. But even this may not be enough information to get a clear picture of people's opinions. The portion of the population that wants to make abortion illegal may be greater or smaller according to the strength of the legal penalty to be applied. In addition, some of the students who want no legal penalty for having an abortion may want strict medical requirements imposed on abortion clinics, while others may not. You will need to design additional specific questions in order to accurately determine respondents' views on these issues.

The number of questions to include in your questionnaire is a matter to be carefully considered. The first general rule, as mentioned earlier, is to ask a sufficient number of questions to find out precisely what it is you want to know. A second principle, however, conflicts with this first rule. This principle, which may not be a problem in your political science class, is that people in general do not like to fill out surveys. Survey information can be very valuable, and pollsters are found on street corners, in airports, and on the telephone. Short surveys with a small number of questions are more likely to be answered completely than long questionnaires. The questionnaire for your paper in survey research methods should normally contain between ten and twenty-five questions.

Surveys consist of two types of questions: closed and open. Closed questions restrict the response of the respondent to a specific set of answers. Many types of closed questions are used in public opinion surveys, but they may be grouped into three categories:

- Two-choice questions
- Three-choice questions
- Multiple-choice questions

Two-choice questions may ask for a simple preference between candidates, such as if the election were held today, for whom would you vote: John McCain or Barack Obama?

Issue-centered two-choice questions offer respondents a choice of one of two answers, most often "yes" and "no," or "agree" and "disagree," as shown below:

Is a mandatory five-day waiting period for the purchase of a handgun desirable?

☐ Yes   ☐ No

A balanced budget amendment to the Constitution should be passed.

☐ Agree   ☐ Disagree

Two-choice questions ask respondents to choose between two statements, neither of which they may entirely support. To find out how many people are ambivalent on these issues, three-choice questions are often asked, giving respondents a third selection, which is most often "undecided," "no opinion," "uncertain," "do not know," "does not apply," or "not sure":

The political party that does the most for Latino people is

☐ Republican   ☐ Democratic   ☐ Uncertain

Simple multiple-choice questions are sometimes constructed to provide a wider range of choices, such as in the following:

If the Republican primary election were held today, for whom would you vote:

☐ Ron Paul   ☐ Scott Brown
☐ Sarah Palin   ☐ Newt Gingrich

Just as often, however, multiple-choice questions are constructed to discriminate more clearly between positions in a range of attitudes. For example, Likert scale multiple-choice questions are used to distinguish among degrees of agreement on a range of possible views on an issue. A Likert-scale question might be stated like this:

"American military expenditures should be reduced by an additional 10 percent to provide funds for domestic programs." Select one of the following responses to this statement:

☐ Strongly agree   ☐ Agree   ☐ Not sure
☐ Disagree   ☐ Strongly disagree

Guttmann-scale multiple-choice questions allow discrimination among a range of answers by creating a series of statements with which it is increasingly difficult to agree or disagree. A respondent who selects one item on the scale of questions is also likely to agree with the items higher on the scale. Consider this example.

Select the answer with which you agree most completely:

1. Citizen ownership of military weapons such as rocket launchers should be restricted.
2. Citizen ownership of fully automatic weapons such as machine guns should be restricted.
3. Citizen ownership of semiautomatic weapons should be restricted.
4. Citizen ownership of handguns and concealed weapons should be restricted.
5. Citizen ownership of hunting rifles should be restricted.

Closed questions have the advantage of being easy to quantify. A number value can be assigned to each answer, and totals can be made of answers of different types.

By contrast, open questions, or open-ended questions, are not easy to quantify. In open questions, respondents are not provided a fixed list of choices but may answer anything they want. The advantage of using open questions is that your survey may discover ideas or attitudes of which you were unaware. Suppose, for example, that you ask the following question and give space for respondents to write their answers:

What should be done about gun control?

You might, for example, get a response like the following:

All firearms should be restricted to law enforcement agencies in populated areas. Special, privately owned depositories should be established for hunters to store their rifles for use in target practice or during hunting season.

Open questions call for a more active and thoughtful response than do closed questions. The fact that more time and effort are required may be a disadvantage because in general the more time and effort a survey demands, the fewer responses it is likely to get. Despite this disadvantage, open questions are to be preferred to closed questions when you want to expand the range of possible answers in order to find out how much diversity there is among opinions on an issue. For practice working with open questions, you should include at least one in your survey questionnaire.

Perhaps the greatest difficulty with asking open questions is that of quantifying the results. The researcher must examine each answer and then group the responses according to their content. For example, responses clearly in favor, clearly opposed, and ambivalent to gun control might be differentiated. Open questions are of particular value to researchers who are doing continuing research over time. The responses they obtain help them to create better questions for their next survey.

In addition to the regular open and closed questions on your survey questionnaire, you will want to add identifiers, which ask for personal information about the respondents, such as gender, age, political party, religion, income level, or other items that may be relevant to the particular topic of your survey. If you ask questions about gun control, for example, you may want to know if men respond differently than women, if Democrats respond differently than Republicans, or if young people respond differently than older people.

Once you have written the survey questionnaire, you need to conduct the survey. You will need to distribute it to the class or other group of respondents. Be sure to provide clear directions for filling out the questionnaire on the survey form. If the students are to complete the survey in class, read out the directions loud and ask if there are any questions before they begin.

10.6   Collect the Data

If your sample is only the size of a small political science class, you will be able to tabulate the answers to the questions directly from the survey form. If you have a larger sample, however, you may want to use data collection forms such as those from the Scantron Corporation. You may be using such forms (on which respondents use a number 2 pencil to mark answers) when you take multiple-choice tests in some of your classes now. The advantage of Scantron forms is that they are processed through computers that tabulate the results and sometimes provide some statistical measurements. If you use Scantron sheets, you will need access to computers that process the results, and you may need someone to program the computer to provide the specific statistical data that you need.

10.7   Analyze the Data

Once you have collected the completed survey forms, you will need to analyze the data that they provide. Statistical procedures are helpful here to perform three tasks:

1. Describe the data
2. Compare components of the data
3. Evaluate the data

There are many statistical procedures especially designed to carry out each of these tasks. This chapter provides only a few examples of the methods that may be used in each category. Consult your instructor or a survey research methods textbook to learn about other types of statistical measurement tools.

Statistics designed to describe data may be very simple. We will start our discussion with two example questions, both employing the Likert scale:

Question 1

"American military expenditures should be reduced by an additional 10 percent to provide funds for domestic programs." Select one of the following responses to this statement:

☐ Strongly agree   ☐ Agree   ☐ Not sure
☐ Disagree   ☐ Strongly disagree

Question 2

"Congress should provide the Department of Defense with more funding for research into germ warfare techniques." Select one of the following responses to this statement:

☐ Strongly agree   ☐ Agree   ☐ Not sure
☐ Disagree   ☐ Strongly disagree

Our objective in describing the data is to see how our hypothetical respondent sample of forty-two students, as a group, answered these questions. The first step is to assign a numerical value to each answer, as follows:

ANSWER	POINTS
Strongly agree	1
Agree	2
Not sure	3
Disagree	4
Strongly disagree	5

Our next step is to count our survey totals to see how many respondents in our hypothetical sample marked each answer to each question:

ANSWER	POINTS	Q1 RESPONSES	Q2 RESPONSES
Strongly agree	1	8	13
Agree	2	16	10
Not sure	3	12	1
Disagree	4	4	12
Strongly disagree	5	2	6

We may now calculate the mean (numerical average) of responses by performing the following operations for each question:

1. Multiply the point value by the number of responses to determine the number of value points.
2. Add the total value points for each answer.
3. Divide the total value points by the number of respondents (forty-two in this case).

To see how this procedure is done, examine the chart below, which analyzes the responses to Question 1. Notice that column 1 contains the answer choices provided to the respondents; column 2 contains the point value assigned to each choice;

column 3 contains the number of respondents who selected each answer; and column 4 contains the value points assigned for each answer choice, multiplied by the number of responses.

VALUE POINTS

ANSWER CHOICES	ASSIGNED POINT VALUE	NUMBER OF RESPONSES	POINT VALUE × NUMBER OF RESPONSES
Strongly agree	1	8	8
Agree	2	16	32
Not sure	3	12	36
Disagree	4	4	16
Strongly disagree	5	2	10
Total	42	102	
Mean			2.43

We can see that there are 42 total responses and 102 total value points. Dividing the number of value points (102) by the total number of responses (42), we get a mean of 2.43.

If we conduct the same operation for the responses to Question 2 in our survey, we get the following results:

VALUE POINTS

ANSWER CHOICES	ASSIGNED POINT VALUE	NUMBER OF RESPONSES	POINT VALUE × NUMBER OF RESPONSES
Strongly agree	1	13	13
Agree	2	10	20
Not sure	3	1	3
Disagree	4	12	48
Strongly disagree	5	6	30
Total		42	114
Mean			2.71

We see from the above table that the mean of the responses for Question 2 is 2.71. Comparing the means of the two questions, we find that the mean for Question 1 (2.43) is lower than the mean for Question 2. Because the lowest value (1 point) is assigned to a response of "strongly agree," and the highest value (5 points) is assigned for a response of "strongly disagree," we know that a high mean score indicates that the sample surveyed tends to disagree with the statement made in the survey question. It is possible to conclude, therefore, that there is slightly more agreement with the statement in Question 1 than with the statement in Question 2. Comparing the mean values in this fashion allows us to easily compare the amount of agreement and disagreement on different questions among the people surveyed.

Another frequently used statistical measure is the standard deviation, which provides a single number that indicates how dispersed the responses to the question are. It tells you, in other words, the extent to which the answers are grouped together at the middle ("agree," "not sure," and "disagree") or are dispersed to the extreme answers ("strongly agree" and "strongly disagree"). To calculate the standard deviation (S) for Question 1, we will follow these steps:

Step 1. Assign a value to each response and the frequency of each response.

Step 2. Find the mean for the question.

Step 3. Subtract the value from the mean.

Step 4. Square the results of Step 3.

Step 5. Multiply the results of Step 4 by the frequency of each value.

Step 6. Sum the values in Step 5.

Step 7. Divide the values in Step 6 by the number of respondents.

Step 8. Find the square root of the value in Step 7, which is the standard deviation.

Our calculation of the standard deviation of Question 1 therefore looks like this:

STEP 1	STEP 2	STEP 3	STEP 4	STEP 5	STEP 6	STEP 7	STEP 8
Value (V) and frequency (F)	Mean	Mean minus value	Step 3 squared	Step 4 times the frequency	Sum of values in Step 5	Step 6 divided by no. of respondents	Square Root of Step 7: Standard Deviation
$V = 1, F = 8$	2.43	1.43	2.04	16.32			
$V = 2, F = 16$	2.43	0.43	0.18	2.88			
$V = 3, F = 12$	2.43	2.57	0.32	3.84			
$V = 4, F = 4$	2.43	21.57	2.46	9.84			
$V = 5, F = 2$	2.43	22.57	6.6	13.2			
					46.08	1.10	1.05

The standard deviation of Question 1 is 1.05. To understand its significance, we need to know that public opinion samples usually correspond to what is known as a normal distribution. In a normal distribution, 68.26 percent of the responses will fall between (1) the mean minus one standard deviation (2.43 − 1.05, or 1.38, in Question 1) and (2) the mean plus one standard deviation (2.43 + 1.05, or 3.48, in Question 1). In other words, in a normal distribution, about two-thirds of the respondents to Question 1 will express an opinion that is between 1.38 and 3.48 on the scale of assigned point values. Another one-third of the respondents will score less than 1.38 or more than 3.48.

For convenience, we will call the responses "strongly agree" and "strongly disagree" as extreme responses, and we will designate "agree," "not sure," and "disagree" as moderate responses. We see that a score of 1.38 is closest to our first extreme, "strongly agree." A score of 3.48 inclines to "disagree," but is "not sure." We may conclude that a substantial portion of the respondents (about one-third) tend to give extreme answers to Question 1. We may also notice that the score 1.38, which indicates strong agreement, is closer to its absolute extreme (1.38 is only 0.38 away from its absolute extreme of 1.0) than is the score 3.48 (which is 1.52 points from its absolute extreme of 5). This means that the responses are slightly more tightly packed toward the extreme of strong agreement. We may conclude that extreme respondents are more likely to strongly agree than to strongly disagree with the statement in Question 1. We can now see more completely the degree of extremism in the population of respondents. Standard deviations become more helpful as the number of the questions in a survey increases because they allow us to compare quickly and easily the extent of extremism in answers. You will find other measures of dispersion in addition to the standard deviation in your statistical methods textbooks.

After finding the amount of dispersion in responses to a question, you may want to see if different types of respondents answered the question in different ways; that is, you may want to measure relationships in the data. For example, from examining our political party identifier, we find, among our respondents to Question 1, fifteen Democrats, fourteen Republicans, and thirteen independents. To compare their responses, we need to construct a correlation matrix that groups responses by identifier:

ANSWER	DEMOCRAT RESPONSES	REPUBLICAN RESPONSES	INDEPENDENT RESPONSES	TOTAL (FREQUENCY)
Strongly agree	4	2	2	8
Agree	8	4	4	16
Not sure	3	5	4	12
Disagree	0	2	2	4
Strongly disagree	0	1	1	2

Each number of responses in the matrix is found in a location known as a response cell. The numbers in the total (frequency) column are known as response total cells. From this matrix, it appears that Democrats are more likely to agree with the question 1 statement than are either Republicans or independents. If this is true for the sample population, there is a correlation between party affiliation and opinion on the issue.

10.8   Include the Elements of a Public Opinion Survey Paper

A public opinion survey paper is composed of five essential parts:

1. Title page
2. Abstract
3. Text
4. Reference page
5. Appendixes

Title Page

The title page should follow the format directions in Chapter 4. The title of a public opinion survey paper should provide the reader with two types of information: the subject of the survey and the population being polled. Examples of titles for papers based on in-class surveys are "University of South Carolina Student Opinions on Welfare Reform," "Ohio Wesleyan University Student Attitudes about Sexual Harassment," and "The 2006 Gubernatorial Election and the Student Vote."

Abstract

Abstracts for a public opinion survey paper should follow the general format directions given for abstracts in Chapter 4. In approximately 100 words, the abstract should summarize the subject, methodology, and results of the survey. An abstract for the example used in this chapter might appear something like this:

A survey of attitudes of college students toward the amount of U.S. military expenditures was undertaken in October 2006 at Western State University. The sample was composed of forty-two students in a political science research methods class. The purpose of the survey was to determine the extent to which students are aware of and concerned about recent defense expenditure reductions, including those directly affecting the Seventh Congressional District, in which the university is located, and to determine student attitudes on related defense questions, such as germ warfare. The results indicate a weak correlation between political party affiliation and attitude toward expenditures, with Democrats favoring reductions more than Republicans.

Text

The text of the paper should include five sections:

1. Introduction
2. Literature review
3. Methodology
4. Results
5. Discussion

Introduction.   The introduction should explain the purpose of your paper, define the research question hypothesis, and describe the circumstances under which the research was conducted. Your purpose statement will normally be a paragraph in which you explain your reasons for conducting your research. You may want to say something like the following:

> The purpose of this paper is to define Howard University student attitudes toward federal student aid programs. In particular, this study seeks to understand how students view the criteria for aid eligibility and the efficiency of application procedures. Further, the survey is expected to indicate the amount of knowledge students have about the federal student aid process. The primary reason for conducting this study is that the results will provide a basis for identifying problems in the aid application and disbursement process, and facilitate discussion among administrative officers and students about solutions to problems that are identified.

Next, the introduction should state the research question and the research hypotheses. The research question in the above example might be "Is student knowledge of federal student aid programs related to student attitudes about the effectiveness of the programs?" A hypothesis might be "Student ratings of the effectiveness of federal student aid programs are positively correlated with student knowledge of the programs."

Literature Review.   A literature review is written to demonstrate that you are familiar with the professional literature relevant to the survey and to summarize that literature for the reader. Your literature review for a public opinion survey paper should address two types of information: the subject and the methodology of the survey.

The subject of the survey, for example, may be a state's proposed secondary education reforms. In this case, the purpose of the subject section of your literature review would be to briefly inform your readers about (1) the history, content, and political implications of the proposed reforms; and (2) the current status of the proposed reforms. In providing this information, you will cite appropriate documents, such as bills submitted to the legislature.

The purpose of the methodology section of your literature review will be to cite the literature that supports the methodology of your study. If you follow the directions in this manual or your course textbook to write your paper, briefly state the procedures and statistical calculations you use in the study and the source of your information (this manual or your text) about them.

Methodology.   The methodology section of your paper describes how you conducted your study. It should first briefly describe the format and content of the questionnaire. For example, how many questions were asked? What kinds of questions (open, closed, Likert scale, Guttmann scale) were used, and why were these formats selected? What identifiers were selected? Why? What topics within the subject matter were given emphasis? Why? Here you should also briefly address the statistical procedures used in data analysis. Why were they selected? What information are they intended to provide?

Results. The results section of your paper should list the findings of your study. Here you report the results of your statistical calculations. You may want to construct a table that summarizes the numbers of responses to each question on the questionnaire. Next, using your statistical results, answer your research question; that is, tell your reader if your research question was answered by your results and, if so, what the answers are.

Discussion. In your discussion section, draw out the implications of your findings. What is the meaning of the results of your study? What conclusions can you draw? What questions remain unanswered? At the end of this section, provide the reader with suggestions for further research that are derived from your research findings.

Reference Page
Your reference page and source citations in the text should be completed according to the directions in Chapter 5.

Appendixes
See Chapter 4 for further directions on placing appendixes at the end of your text. Appendixes for a public opinion survey paper should include the following:

- A copy of the questionnaire used in the study
- Tables of survey data not sufficiently important to be included in the text but helpful for reference
- Summaries of survey data from national polls on the same subject, if such polls are available and discussed in your text.

- **Note:** Students and instructors should note that the applications of the mean and standard deviation suggested in this chapter are controversial because they are applied to ordinal data. In practice, however, such applications are common.

CHAPTER 11

Domestic and International Policy Analysis Papers

11.1   Learn the Basics of Policy Analysis

What is Policy Analysis?

When President Obama took office he faced a long list of problems, some of which seemed almost over-powering. The nation was in the trough of its deepest recession since the Great Depression of the 1930s. America was fighting wars in both Iraq and Afghanistan. The health care system was the worst among the world's great powers. Hundreds of thousands of medical bankruptcies, gaps in health insurance coverage, and soaring medical costs were three of the many challenges to be faced. Governments solve problems by formulating *policies*, which are sets of principles or rules that guide government agencies in creating and running programs aimed at dealing with the problems. Confronted with a vast array of serious national predicaments, President Obama's administration developed and proposed to Congress a set of policies, some of which were eventually passed and became law.

Domestic policies include matters *within* nations, such as highways, hospitals, schools, water treatment plants, law enforcement, public safety and many other issues. International policies affect relations *between or among* nations, such as trade, war, educational exchanges, disaster relief efforts, and so on.

Policy analysis is the examination of a policy (domestic or international) to determine its *effectiveness* (how well it solves the problem it was designed to solve) and its *efficiency* (the extent to which the cost of implementing the policy is reasonable, considering the size and nature of the problem to be solved). Every day at all levels of government, analysts, sometimes called policy wonks, are writing policy analysis papers. Legislators at the state and national levels hire staff people who continually investigate public policy issues and seek ways to improve legislated policy. At the national level, the Congressional Research Service continually finds information for representatives and senators. Each committee of Congress employs staff members who help it review current laws and define options for making new ones. State legislatures also employ their own research agencies and committee staff. Legislators and other policymakers are also given policy information by hundreds of public interest groups and research organizations.

Public officials are constantly challenged to initiate new policies or change old ones. If they have a current formal policy at all, they want to know how effective it is. They then want to know what options are available to them, what changes they might make to improve current policy, and what the consequences of those changes will be. Policies are reviewed under a number of circumstances. Policy analyses are sometimes conducted as part of the normal agency budgeting processes. They help decision makers determine what policies should be continued or discontinued. These policies under scrutiny may be very narrow in scope, such as deciding the hours of operation of facilities at city parks, or they may be very broad, such as deciding how the nation will provide health care or defense for its citizens.

In writing a policy analysis paper, you should:

1. Select and clearly define a specific government policy.
2. Carefully define the social, governmental, economic, or other problem which the policy is designed to solve.
3. Describe the economic, social, and political environments in which the problem arose and in which the existing policy for solving the problem was developed.
4. Evaluate the effectiveness of the current policy or lack of policy in dealing with the problem.
5. Identify alternative policies that could be adopted to solve the selected problem, and estimate the economic, social, environmental, and political costs and benefits of each alternative.
6. Provide a summary comparison of all policies examined.

Successful policy analysis papers all share the same general purpose: to inform policymakers about how public policy in a specific area may be improved. A policy analysis paper, like a position paper, is an entirely practical exercise. It is neither theoretical nor general. Its objective is to identify and evaluate the policy options that are available for a specific topic.

11.2 Write a Policy Analysis Paper

The Contents of a Policy Analysis Paper

Policy analysis papers contain six basic elements:

1. Title page
2. Executive summary
3. Table of contents, including a list of tables and illustrations
4. Text (or body)
5. References to sources of information
6. Appendixes

Parameters of the Text

Ask your instructor for the number of pages required for the policy analysis paper assigned for your course. Such papers at the undergraduate level often range from twenty to fifty typed, double-spaced pages in length.

Two general rules govern the amount of information presented in the body of the paper. First, content must be adequate to make a good policy evaluation. You must include all the facts necessary to understand the significant strengths and weaknesses of a policy and its alternatives. If your paper omits a fact that is critical to the decision, a poor decision will likely be made.

Never omit important facts merely because they tend to support a perspective other than your own. It is your responsibility to present the facts as clearly as possible, not to bias the evaluation in a particular direction.

The second guideline for determining the length of a policy analysis paper is to omit extraneous material. Include only the information that is helpful in making the particular decision at hand. If, for example, you are analyzing the policy by which a municipal government funds a museum dedicated to the history of fishing in area lakes, how much information do you need to include about the specific exhibits in the museum?

The Format of a Policy Analysis Paper

Title Page.   The title page for a policy analysis paper should follow the format provided for title pages in Chapter 4.

Executive Summary.   A one-page, single-spaced executive summary immediately follows the title page. The carefully written sentences of the executive summary express the central concepts to be explained more fully in the text of the paper. The purpose of the summary is to allow the decision maker to understand, as quickly as possible, the major facts and issues under consideration. The decision maker should be able to get a clear and thorough overview of the entire policy problem and the value and costs of available policy options by reading the one-page summary.

Table of Contents.   The table of contents of a policy analysis paper must follow the organization of the paper's text and should conform to the format shown in Chapter 4.

Text.   The structure of a policy analysis paper's text may be outlined as follows.

I. Description of the policy currently in force
   A. A clear, concise statement of the policy currently in force
   B. A brief history of the policy currently in force
   C. A description of the problem the current policy was aimed at resolving, including an estimate of its extent and importance
II. Environments of the policy currently in force
   A. A description of the *physical* factors affecting the origin, development, and implementation of the current policy
   B. A description of the *social* factors affecting the origin, development, and implementation of the current policy
   C. A description of the *economic* factors affecting the origin, development, and implementation of the current policy
   D. A description of the *political* factors affecting the origin, development, and implementation of the current policy

III. **Effectiveness and efficiency of the current policy**
  A. How well the existing policy does what it was designed to do
  B. How well the policy performs in relation to the effort and resources committed to it
IV. **Policy alternatives**
  A. Possible alterations of the present policy, with the estimated costs and benefits of each
  B. Alternatives to the present policy, with the estimated costs and benefits of each
  V. **Summary comparison of policy options**

Most public policy analysis textbooks describe in detail each of the policy analysis components listed in the above outline. The following sections of this chapter, however, provide further information with respect to section II of this outline. Be sure to discuss the outline with your instructor to ensure that you understand what each entails.

References.   You must be sure to cite properly all sources of information in a policy analysis paper. Follow the directions for proper citation in Chapter 5.

Appendixes.   Appendixes can provide the reader of policy analysis papers with information that supplements the important facts contained in the text. For many local development and public works projects, a map and a diagram are often very helpful appendixes. You should attach them to the end of the paper, after the reference page. You should not append entire government reports, journal articles, or other publications, but feel free to include selected charts, graphs, or other pages. The source of the information should always be evident on the appended pages.

11.3   Analyze a Domestic Policy

The main difference between a typical domestic policy analysis paper and an international policy analysis paper is the range of factors each considers under section II of the outline given above, "Environments of the policy currently in force." We shall now re-examine this section of the outline and provide more detailed directions specifically for domestic policy papers.

Since it is often helpful to use an example when describing policy matters, let's suppose that you decide to write a policy analysis about President Obama's proposal to upgrade passenger rail service within the United States. Your paper will analyze current national policy toward rail service, and you will consider President Obama's proposal as an alternative to the current policy. With respect to current passenger rail service, American policy for the last several decades has been comprised primarily of support for two activities: (1) AMTRAK, and (2) grants to cities to assist in the development of light rail systems. In 2009, President Obama proposed allocating $13 billion to develop a new high-speed rail system that would connect the nation's largest metropolitan areas.

II. **Environments of the policy currently in force**
   A. *A description of the physical factors affecting the origin, development, and implementation of the current policy.* Physical factors to consider in your analysis of passenger rail transportation may include such items as the following:
   - The extent and condition of railroad tracks across the country
   - The extent and condition of railroad cars across the country
   - The extent and condition of railroad stations across the country
   - The extent and condition of railroad support and supply facilities across the country
   - The availability of land for track, cars, stations and other facilities
   - The environmental impact of increasing passenger rail service
   B. *A description of the social factors affecting the origin, development, and implementation of the current policy.* As you gather information for your analysis of passenger rail transportation you may well need to consider these populations within the country:
   - The groups (geographic, ethnic, economic) of people most likely to benefit from a new rail system
   - The groups of people most likely not to benefit from a new rail system
   - The groups of people most likely to experience negative consequences from a new rail system
   C. *A description of the economic factors affecting the origin, development, and implementation of the current policy.* Your analysis of passenger rail transportation may require you to identify and discuss the following economic factors:
   - Those sectors of the economy (tourism, suburban development) that will benefit from upgrading a rail system
   - Those sectors of the economy (automobiles, busses) that will experience negative effects from upgrading a rail system
   - The effects that an upgraded passenger rail systems may have on the nation as a whole
   - How the country will pay for any new developments and who will save or earn money from them
   D. *A description of the political factors affecting the origin, development, and implementation of the current policy.* In your analysis of passenger rail transportation policy analysis you will need to identify and elaborate on such political factors as these:
   - People and organizations likely to support new rail development, and the political power they are able to command
   - People and organizations likely to oppose new rail development, and how effective they might be in their opposition
   - The degree of support and opposition to the policy among members of Congress
   - The degree of general public support and opposition there is for passenger rail improvement

11.4   Analyze a Foreign Policy

Papers analyzing international policy issues—issues that occur substantially between and among nations—should proceed, much like domestic policy analysis papers, according to the outline presented in the foregoing section. One difference between domestic and international policy papers is that in Section I. B. of international policy papers you will provide first a brief history of the country or countries involved in the policy issue you are analyzing, and then a brief history of the current problem or dispute.

But the main difference between the two types of papers is the range of factors they consider under section II of the outline, "Environments of the policy currently in force." Having looked at how section II of the outline helps to shape a typical domestic policy analysis paper, we will now explore how that section of the outline operates for an international policy analysis, and, as before, we will construct an example. Let's suppose that you have decided to write a policy analysis about the Obama administration's support for sanctions against Iran due to that country's suspected development of nuclear weapons. Your paper will analyze both the extent of the threat that Iranian nuclear weapons would pose and the options available to the Obama administration in meeting its goal of deterring Iran from developing nuclear offensive capability.

Note that the following outline, developed from section II of the general outline provided above, makes use of many political concepts not defined in this chapter. These concepts will be well covered in your international relations text, and you will find definitions of them in the Glossary at the end of this manual.

II. **Environments of the policy currently in force**
   A. *A description of the physical factors affecting the origin, development, and implementation of the current policy.* Physical factors to discuss in your analysis of the development of Iranian nuclear weapons might include these:
   - Iran's geographic position in the world
   - The countries that border Iran
   - Strategically important countries in the region (Israel, Russia, etc.)
   - Iran's chief natural resources
   - Factors, such as ports, railways, and mountain ranges, that create either special advantages or disadvantages for Iran
   - Factors tending to make Iran either especially powerful or vulnerable
   B. *A description of the social factors affecting the origin, development, and implementation of the current policy.* Social factors to consider in your analysis of the development of Iranian nuclear weapons might include the following:
   - Dominant ethnic groups
   - Language (Farsi, not Arabic!)
   - Religions
   - Customs and traditions

C. *A description of the economic factors affecting the origin, development, and implementation of the current policy.* Your analysis of the development of Iranian nuclear weapons will need to explore such economic factors as the following:
- The level of Iran's economic development
- Commerce
- Iran's national wealth and debt
- Agriculture
- Banking
- Iran's currency
- Iran's natural resources
- The country's economic class system

D. *A description of the political factors affecting the origin, development, and implementation of the current policy.* The number of political factors affecting the development of an international policy is normally substantial, so the analyst's key chore is to identify the most important ones. Because many issues are so complex that it difficult to know where to start, we suggest that you first organize your survey of potential factors into three broad categories:
- The politics of the international political system
- The domestic politics of the states involved
- The politics of the specific policy issue (in our example, Iranian development of nuclear weapons)

For each of these categories you will want to examine a number of factors. The entries below are by no means exhaustive, and each has a technical meaning within the specific discipline of International Relations (IR). You will find definitions and explanations of each entry in your IR textbook. For your convenience, we list here some of the most important entries in each category to help you begin a systematic review.

The Politics of the International Political System.   What are the characteristics of the current international system? Is it unipolar, bipolar, multipolar? How are the states involved in the issue under study affected by this system? Is there a defined international regime? What factors affect the distribution of power within the international system? What international organizations, both governmental and nongovernmental (NGOs), are important in this particular issue? What processes (globalization, interdependence) play a key role? What formal and informal arrangements control interactions in the system (balances of power, issue linkages, terrorism)?

Domestic Politics of the States Involved.   What are the key political characteristics of the states involved in this issue? What are their formal governmental structures? What are their formal and informal power structures? What internal forces shape the issue and politics in general within the states involved (nationalism, democratization, militarization, structural violence, fragmentation, religious authorities, druglords or warlords, ethnic rivalries)? What doctrines affect the issue (flexible response, protectionism, preemption)?

Politics of the Specific Policy Issue. In our example of the Iranian development of nuclear weapons, several aspects of the specific policy issue readily come to mind:

Iranian national pride

American security and the imperative of nonproliferation

The American-Israeli alliance

Islamic Anti-Americanism

Iranian modernization and pro-Americanism

Russian dependence on Iranian oil

Of course, this is only the start of a list of relevant subtopics for this particular issue. As your research proceeds you will gradually form an impression of the major factors in the issue you are studying and how they relate to one another. As you continue to follow the policy analysis outline provided earlier in this chapter, you will in the end produce the sort of analysis prepared by many people in governments and NGOs every day.

CHAPTER 12

Analyze a Bill Currently Before Congress

The process of examining a bill under consideration by the legislature can teach us many things about how our government works and how those currently serving it think. Accessing the work of legislators, as we will discover, is simple. But finding work of value—a substantive bill that will reward our in-depth consideration—may, unfortunately, prove a more difficult task.

12.1   Select a Substantive Bill to Analyze

Vital though the work of Congress is to the life of the nation, it is an unfortunate fact that many of the pieces of legislation submitted before either of its houses during the course of a typical session will seem to sizable portions of the country to be frivolous. A little experiment will demonstrate how a single topic can generate both serious, useful bills and bills that seem clearly to be a waste of time. Take out your iPhone or Blackberry and open Safari or whatever browser you have. Enter the following address: http://thomas.loc.gov. The online home of the Library of Congress—named in honor of Thomas Jefferson, whose gift to the nation of his own personal library formed the foundation of the Library of Congress—this Web site is the best place on the net to find information about what bills (proposed laws) are currently going through Congress. You will see a line in bold print: **Search Bill Summary and Status**. This search engine allows you to pick any topic you like and find a list of current bills on that topic.

Let's choose an important topic for our experiment. One of the traditional formulations of American values is an old phrase, cherished by some, parodied by others: "God, Mom, and apple pie." Let's see what Congress is doing for Mom. On the day of this writing, when we type "mother" into the search engine we find no fewer than 39 bills now before Congress that have to do with mothers. Try it now and see what you find. It is likely that the list you uncover will resemble the one we have found today.

Looking at the list of bills brought up by our search, we soon realize that there are substantive bills—bills thoughtfully designed to improve the lives of American mothers and, subsequently, the lives of all Americans—and nonsubstantive bills. A nonsubstantive bill is one that doesn't actually do anything. Our list of 39 entries (the list keeps changing as bills go through Congress) contains several like the following. In which category—substantive or nonsubstantive—would you place this one?

> **5.** H.RES.1351 : Congratulating Dallas Braden and the Oakland Athletics baseball team for pitching a perfect game against the Tampa Bay Rays on Mother's Day, May 9, 2010.
>
> **Sponsor:** Rep Stark, Fortney Pete [CA-13] (introduced 5/12/2010)   Cosponsors (17)
>
> **Committees:** House Oversight and Government Reform
>
> **Latest Major Action:** 5/12/2010 Referred to House committee. Status: Referred to the House Committee on Oversight and Government Reform.

At a time when the United States is engaged in two wars, is grappling with the worst economic recession since the Great Depression, and is facing a host of other serious problems, Fortney Pete Stark, representing California's 13th District in the House of Representatives, has chosen to send to the House Oversight and Government Reform Committee, thereby requiring action from at least several of his colleagues, a resolution acknowledging the coincidence of a notable baseball game taking place on Mother's Day.

Most of the "bills" that go through Congress are nonsubstantive. They actually do absolutely nothing. Representative Stark has merely provided us with one example of the hundreds of measures passed by Congress every year with one simple goal of its sponsor in mind: to impress a tiny number of influential constituents (in some cases, only one or two).

Let's go further down our list and see if we can find a substantive bill, one that actually might, if passed, accomplish something other than making its author look like he or she is wasting the taxpayer's time and money.

> **11.** H.R.605 : Pregnant Women Support Act
>
> **Sponsor:** Rep Davis, Lincoln [TN-4] (introduced 1/16/2009)   Cosponsors (6)
>
> **Committees:** House Energy and Commerce; House Ways and Means; House Education and Labor; House Agriculture
>
> **Latest Major Action:** 4/23/2009 Referred to House subcommittee. Status: Referred to the Subcommittee on Department Operations, Oversight, Nutrition and Forestry.

If we click on the hyperlink number of the bill (H.R. 605) we find the following chart:

All Information (except text)	Text of Legislation	CRS Summary	Major Congressional Actions
Titles	Cosponsors (6)	Committees	All Congressional Actions
Related Bills	Amendments	Related Committee Documents	All Congressional Actions with Amendments
CBO Cost Estimates	Subjects		With links to *Congressional Record* pages, votes, reports

If we select <u>CRS Summary</u>, we find a summary of what this bill will do if it is passed:

PREGNANT WOMEN SUPPORT ACT -
AUTHORIZES THE SECRETARY OF HEALTH AND
HUMAN SERVICES TO MAKE GRANTS TO
INCREASE PUBLIC AWARENESS OF RESOURCES
AVAILABLE TO PREGNANT WOMEN TO CARRY
THEIR PREGNANCY TO TERM AND NEW PARENTS.

AMENDS THE PUBLIC HEALTH SERVICE ACT TO
ALLOW THE SECRETARY TO MAKE GRANTS FOR
THE PURCHASE OF ULTRASOUND EQUIPMENT
FOR EXAMINATIONS OF PREGNANT WOMEN.

PROHIBITS A HEALTH INSURANCE ISSUER
OFFERING INDIVIDUAL COVERAGE FROM
IMPOSING A PREEXISTING CONDITION EXCLUSION
OR A WAITING PERIOD OR OTHERWISE
DISCRIMINATING AGAINST A WOMAN ON THE
BASIS THAT SHE IS PREGNANT.

PROVIDES FOR CONTINUATION COVERAGE FOR
NEWBORNS.

AMENDS TITLE XXI (STATE CHILDREN'S HEALTH
INSURANCE PROGRAM) (SCHIP) OF THE SOCIAL
SECURITY ACT TO ALLOW STATES TO EXTEND
HEALTH CARE COVERAGE TO AN UNBORN CHILD.

REQUIRES HEALTH FACILITIES THAT PERFORM
ABORTIONS TO OBTAIN INFORMED CONSENT
FROM A PREGNANT WOMAN SEEKING AN
ABORTION.

PROVIDES FOR THE COLLECTION AND
DISSEMINATION OF INFORMATION ON DOWN
SYNDROME AND OTHER PRENATALLY
DIAGNOSED CONDITIONS.

DIRECTS THE SECRETARY TO PROVIDE FOR: (1)
HIGHER EDUCATION PREGNANT AND PARENTING
STUDENT SERVICES OFFICES; AND (2) PROGRAMS
TO WORK WITH PREGNANT OR PARENTING TEENS
TO COMPLETE HIGH SCHOOL.

AUTHORIZES GRANTS FOR SERVICES TO
PREGNANT WOMEN WHO ARE VICTIMS OF
DOMESTIC VIOLENCE, DATING VIOLENCE, OR
STALKING. REQUIRES STATES TO REQUIRE A
PREGNANCY DETERMINATION FOR HOMICIDE
VICTIMS.

REQUIRES THE SECRETARY TO PROVIDE FOR
COMPREHENSIVE AND SUPPORTIVE SERVICES
FOR PREGNANT WOMEN, **MOTHERS**, AND
CHILDREN.

AMENDS THE INTERNAL REVENUE CODE TO
INCREASE AND MAKE REFUNDABLE THE TAX
CREDIT FOR ADOPTION EXPENSES.

AUTHORIZES APPROPRIATIONS TO CARRY OUT
THE SPECIAL SUPPLEMENTAL NUTRITION
PROGRAM FOR WOMEN, INFANTS, AND
CHILDREN (WIC PROGRAM).

AMENDS THE FOOD STAMP ACT OF 1977 TO
INCREASE THE ELIGIBILITY THRESHOLD FOR
FOOD STAMPS.

AUTHORIZES APPROPRIATIONS TO CARRY OUT
THE CHILD CARE AND DEVELOPMENT BLOCK
GRANT ACT OF 1990.

AUTHORIZES GRANTS TO PROVIDE TO ELIGIBLE
MOTHERS EDUCATION ON THE HEALTH NEEDS
OF THEIR INFANTS THROUGH VISITS TO THEIR
HOMES BY REGISTERED NURSES.

AUTHORIZES GRANTS FOR COLLECTING AND
REPORTING ABORTION SURVEILLANCE
DATA.

Whether you approve or disapprove of what this bill does, it clearly aims to accomplish a lot of tasks. A substantive bill, again, is a bill that *does* something. Find such a bill for a topic that engages your own interests and imagination. Here's a tip that may be helpful to you. Select a bill that has passed through several stages of development rather than one that is brand new. There is usually more information available to you about more mature bills than there is for new bills.

12.2   Follow Six Steps for Writing the Bill Analysis Paper

Once you have found a substantive and interesting bill, follow these six steps in writing your analysis:

1. Create a short summary of the bill you have selected.
2. Identify and evaluate support for this bill.
3. Identify and evaluate opposition to this bill.
4. Describe the legislative process of this bill.
5. Summarize the substantive effects of this legislation.
6. Explain the political implications of this proposed law.

1. Create a Short Summary of the Bill You Have Selected.   The summary should include a single clear, concise paragraph explaining what the bill actually does. For the bill concerning the Pregnant Women Support Act, a summary might look like this:

> The Pregnant Women Support Act (H.R. 605) authorizes the Secretary of Health and Human Services to provide and publicize a variety of new resources for pregnant women and their unborn children. It expands grants for (1) ultrasounds and examinations, (2) new studies of pregnancy-related adverse conditions, (3) services to victims of violence, and (4) mother and child nutrition. It expands public and private insurance coverage for pregnancy-related health, provides support for teen mothers' health and education, encourages adoption, and requires informed consent before abortions.

2. Identify and Evaluate Support for this Bill.   Many people are involved in the process a bill goes through in order to become a law. Legislators are assisted and accosted by dozens of lobbyists, government agency employees, private advocacy groups, and political organizations of all sorts. Probably the best way to get a handle on all this activity is to divide participants into supporters and opponents of the particular bill. Write several paragraphs in which you describe members of Congress, lobbyists, government agencies, private organizations and important individuals who support this bill. Who are the most powerful interested parties? The least powerful? What do particular groups want? Who are the main beneficiaries and how much political influence do they have?

Two sources of information are important for completing this task. First, on the Thomas home page you will find a link to the *Congressional Record*, the official written record, mandated in the U.S. Constitution, of all the bills that go through Congress. The *Congressional Record* includes not only bills but also speeches by members, documents submitted supporting and opposing each bill, transcripts of committee hearings, and much other pertinent information. The second important source is, of course, your online search engine, Google, perhaps, or one of its competitors. You can search by the bill's name or number, or both.

3. Identify and Evaluate Opposition to This Bill.   Write several paragraphs in which you describe members of Congress, lobbyists, government agencies, private organizations and important individuals who have voiced or are likely to voice opposition to this bill, in the same manner as you have completed step 3.

4. Describe the Legislative Process of this Bill. After perusing Thomas, the *Congressional Record*, and the material you have located through the use of your online search engine, provide a brief description of each of the following:

- The Introduction of the Bill. By whom and when was the bill was introduced in Congress?
- The Committee Process. To what committee was it assigned? Were hearings held? What happened at the hearings? What action has the committee taken?
- Floor action. Was the bill debated? What was the content and tone of the debate? What issues surfaced? Did the President or other powerful people intervene? If so, what was the effect of their intervention?
- Conference Committee Action. Because a bill must pass both houses in identical form in order to become law, a committee composed of members of both houses creates a compromise bill from the ones from each house. What effect did the Conference Committee's compromise have on the bill?
- Presidential Action. Has the bill been sent to the White House? Has the President responded?

5. Summarize the Substantive Effects of This Legislation. In a few paragraphs, explain what difference in the lives of Americans this bill will make if it is passed. Whom will it affect? Make both quantitative and qualitative evaluations. Will it affect a few people greatly, a lot of people in a minor way, a few people marginally? Or will it significantly change the lives of large numbers of Americans? How positive will these effects be? Will there be significant side effects to the bill? Consider social and economic impacts of the bill.

6. Explain the Political Implications of This Proposed Law. What interest groups will win or lose if this bill is passed? Will either of the two major political parties derive benefits? Will particular politicians gain or lose influence if this act is passed? As you conclude your analysis, provide your own assessment of the extent to which this bill will improve America's future.

CHAPTER **13**
Compare Political Systems

13.1   Learn How to Compare Political Systems

You are off to a good start. You have made a very wise choice: you have opted to study comparative politics, and there are few more challenging, rewarding, and beneficial subjects in any discipline. Comparative politics is the most promising key to answering some of the most pressing questions in the world today. What kind of government is most likely to survive the violence in Iraq? How can the people of Afghanistan, who have had little experience with democracy, come to appreciate it, and apply it to their own benefit, and help it withstand the brutal totalitarian violence of the Taliban? You will grapple with these and many similar vital questions in the course of your studies.

As you are writing a paper for a course in comparative politics your text has already introduced you to what this fascinating subdiscipline is all about, and so this chapter will help you apply what you know so far to making the decisions that will produce a meaningful and beneficial paper.

As mentioned in previous chapters, let us start with the basics. Most simply, what do comparative political scientists do? Three things. They collect data, analyze it, and interpret it. This sounds simple, and as a linear process, it is. A linear process is one in which the steps simply follow each other, one at a time. The comparative politics process, however, is more complex than that. Each of the three steps is in tension with each other and constantly affects the other two. For example, as you analyze the data you find that you do not have enough information, and so you go back and collect more. Again, as you interpret the data you find that your analysis is deficient, so you go back and employ additional statistical techniques, and so on. This complex process is sometimes referred to as being recursive because, as opposed to being a simple linear progression from one step to another, it involves complex interactions among the three basic steps in the process. The comparative political science process, then, might be portrayed like this:

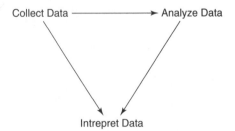

We may say, then, that comparative politics can be described as a recursive process of data collection, analysis, and interpretation that helps us understand a wide array of political, social, economic, cultural events, practices, and other phenomena around the world.

To provide some context for the task you are about to undertake, it may be helpful to know that on the professional level, there are two main groups of comparative politics professionals: practitioners and academics. Literally hundreds of people in the United States alone—employees of the Departments of State and Commerce, the intelligence agencies, and the military to name a few—are active practitioners of the profession of comparative politics. They practice their profession in two ways. First, they produce data about elections, parties, movements, and many other phenomena that they and others can analyze. Second, they continually read studies written by other practitioners and academics, looking for information that helps them solve the problems they are working on. They then apply this information in actual situations, such as in negotiating, tracking political movements, or in moderating disputes among other nations.

Academic comparativists are found in universities and research institutes. What is the cutting edge of academic comparative political science? Work in recent decades has become increasingly theoretical and quantitative. In a recent overview of his sub-discipline, Stanford political scientist David D. Laitin describes the recent emergence of a "new consensus" among academic comparativists that embraces a "tripartite methodology," which explains how they collect, analyze, and interpret data.

The first part of the tripartite methodology employs a variety of *cross-sectional* and *diachronic* statistical techniques. Cross-sectional studies select certain aspects of politics, such as the structure of nations' political economy, the variety and ideologies of political parties, or the concentrations of power among elites, and then compare how these factors affect political developments from one nation to another. Cross-sectional studies often *compare large numbers of nations.* Diachronic studies examine how things such as methods of building consensus, techniques of conflict resolution, or concentrations of power develop *over specific periods of time.*

The second of the three methods is *formalization*, which means the development and testing of formal models. Formal models are complex statistical methodologies, some borrowed and modified from the study of *econometrics*, that explain or predict the effects that certain variables (such as substantial immigration, recession, or expansion of the right to vote) have on political systems.

The third component of Laitin's tripartite methodology is *narrative*. Narratives, most simply, are stories. In comparative political science, however, the word narrative has a more specific meaning. Political science narratives are attempts to explain what the data means, and what conclusions can be drawn from it. Are there anomalies (discrepancies or contradictions) in the statistical results? What can explain them? Does the data support or refute particular current theories about how people interact in specific political situations? These questions and many more are addressed in comparative political narratives.

13.2   Learn to Think Comparatively

In this chapter, you will find directions for how to write an elementary cross-sectional paper. It will be a cross-sectional study because you will select certain aspects of politics, and then compare how these factors affect phenomena in more than one country. It will be elementary because (1) you will not be collecting original data yourself, but you will be using data collected by other people, (2) you will not construct or apply formal models, and (3) the statistics you employ will be relatively simple. The purpose of your paper will be to compare the relationship between two political variables as these two variables interact with each other within the three different countries. The information below will explain how to select appropriate variables and countries for your study.

You will find it most helpful to go to your college library's Web page and browse some articles in academic comparative politics journals before your start your paper. In Appendix A of this manual you will find a list of more than 200 academic journals that publish articles in political science, including journals specifically dedicated to comparative studies, such as *Comparative Political Studies*, *Comparative Politics*, *Comparative Strategy*, and *Comparative Studies in Society and History*. You will also find numerous journals that specialize in area studies, such as *Asian Affairs*, *Atlantic Community Quarterly*, *East European Quarterly*, *Modern China*, and *Pacific Affairs*. By browsing recent articles, you will quickly gain a better understanding of what comparative political scientist study is, the methods they use, and what they have learned. You can also find many, if not most, of these journals online through your college library Internet portal.

13.3   Follow Eight Steps for Writing an Elementary Cross-Sectional Comparative Politics Paper

Writing your cross-sectional study will require completing the following eight steps.

1. Select the variables you wish to study.
2. Select the countries you wish to study.
3. Conduct a literature review.
4. Formulate a research question and a hypothesis.
5. Adopt or construct a methodology.
6. Collect Data.
7. Analyze Data.
8. Compose the narrative (thesis).

Step 1. Select the Variables You Wish to Study.   You have a wide array of variables to choose from and it is always a good idea to consult with your instructor for assistance in selecting and defining variables in a manner most likely to produce interesting and significant results. Although an exhaustive list would be far more extensive, you may find the Chart of Comparative Political Phenomena (below) to be useful. Here you will find several different categories of variables that comparative political scientists often study and examples of variables within each category that you might find interesting.

CHART OF POLITICAL PHENOMENA

CATEGORY	VARIABLE	MEANING OR EFFECT OF VARIABLE
Power	Possession and exclusion	Who wields power, and who is excluded from it?
	Concentration and dispersion	To what extent is power concentrated and dispersed?
	Legitimacy and corruption	To what extent is existing power perceived to be legitimate or corrupt?
Nation States	Nationalism	How strong is national sentiment overall? In what groups is it strongest and weakest?
	Cohesion	To what extent do the political, social, and economic structures and processes result in a strong, cohesive state?
	Environment	How do the state's neighbors, region, and the international system as a whole affect its vitality?
Institutions	Legislative	Who makes the laws, and what are the processes by which the laws are made?
	Executive	Who carries out the laws? How effective is the execution of the laws?
	Judicial	Who interprets the laws? What role does the judiciary play in the politics of the state?
	Bureaucracy	How is the bureaucracy organized and led? How effective and efficient is it? How corrupt is it?
	Military	How large, strong, well-armed, and effective is the military? What political role does it play?
	Mediating	What institutions (such as churches, social clubs, labor and unions) play a mediating role between the government and the people? How effective are they?
Democracy	Constitution and structure	How democratic are the constitution and the legally constituted structures and procedures of government?
	Processes	To what extent do processes designed to provide democracy actually succeed in doing so?
	Values	How much and what kinds of freedom, justice, and equality actually exist in the society?
Participation	Election process	How numerous, frequent, and open are the elections?
	Election participation	How many people participate? What groups participate more than others?
	Political parties	How many political parties exist, and what ideological, ethnic, and economic interests do they represent?

(Continued)

CHART OF POLITICAL PHENOMENA *(Continued)*

CATEGORY	VARIABLE	MEANING OR EFFECT OF VARIABLE
	Interest groups	What are the major influential interest groups, and what interests do they represent?
	Movements	Do any influential social or political movements exist? What effect do they have?
	Dissent	To what extent is dissent tolerated? How much dissent is currently expressed and how is it expressed?
Political Culture	Traditions	What are the society's major politically relevant traditions and customs?
	Ethnicity	What are the major ethnic groups, and what role do they play in politics?
	Religion	What are the major religions, and what role do they play in politics?
	Education	What are the extent and quality of education? How does the educational system affect politics?
Ideology	Liberalism	How are liberals and conservatives defined within this society? How strong is each group?
	Socialism	To what extent does the government own the country's means of production? How influential are socialist parties and groups?
	Authoritarian and totalitarian	To what extent do authoritarian and/or totalitarian ideologies influence power structures and policies?
Economy	Industry	What are the extent, content, and influence of the country's industrial base?
	Commerce	What are the extent, content, and influence of the country's commercial enterprises?
	Resources	What are the country's major resources? Who controls them?
	Development	What is the overall status of the country's economic development?

From the above list (or any other list of variables agreed upon in consultation with your instructor) select two variables that you believe might affect each other. For example, you might be interested in studying the relationship between religion and political cohesion. You may want to determine the extent to which certain religions contribute to or detract from the political cohesion of different societies.

Step 2. Select the Countries You Wish to Study. The second step is to select three countries in which to examine the relationship between the two variables you have selected. For the purposes of this class assignment you will probably find it is a good idea to select three countries that are geographically similar (contiguous if possible) and that are in at least one variable. For example, if the two variables are religion and cohesion, you may want to pick three countries that are all predominantly Muslim, and all in the Middle East. By doing this you will reduce the number of intervening variables that may affect your result.

Step 3. Conduct a Literature Review. See Chapter 9 of this manual for some general directions on how to conduct a literature review. Remember that you are not just looking for information about the countries and variables you are studying, but you are also looking for information on the variables you have selected, and on methodologies that have been employed to study those variables. So, following the example we are using, in this case, you will be particularly interested in finding information on (1) the relationship between religion and social cohesion in general, (2) the relationship between Islam and cohesion in particular, and (3) methodologies that have been used to determine the relationship between religion and cohesion.

Although you may find some good sources using Google or Yahoo, you will find far better quality of information about substantive topics such as methodologies and religions by using the academic databases subscribed to by your university or college. Among the more promising of these will be JSTOR and EBSCOHOST. For a wide variety of information about the countries you will be studying, these Web sites are good places to start:

U.S. Department of State—Countries—Background Notes:

http://www.state.gov/r/pa/ei/bgn/

Central Intelligence Agency—The World Fact Book:

https://www.cia.gov/cia/publications/factbook/index.html

United Nations—InfoNation:

http://www.un.org/Pubs/CyberSchoolBus/infonation3/menu/advanced.asp

Step 4. Formulate a Research Question and a Hypothesis. Comparative politics text provides you with information about research questions and hypotheses in comparative politics, so we shall not repeat that information here. It is sufficient for our purposes to remember that a research question is a clear statement of what you are attempting to find out in your study. Using our example, a research question for our paper might be:

How does the religion of Islam affect the internal political cohesion of Egypt, Libya, and Tunisia?

A hypothesis is an educated guess about what your research will ultimately discover. Making such guesses helps you focus more clearly on what you want to discover. A hypothesis for our example paper might be:

While moderate Muslims contribute to political cohesion, radical Muslims detract from it.

Step 5. Construct or Adopt a Methodology. This may be the most difficult part of your study. First, you will have to identify what you intend to measure. In this case of our example, you will have to define "political cohesion," in such a way that you can identify quantifiable measures of it. One such measure might be "number and extent of incidents of political violence." Another might be "strength and number of separatist movements." You should identify at least three to six measures of each variable.

Step 6. Data Collection.   Next, you will need to identify sources of data. The sources listed in the Literature Review section (Step 3) will probably be a good place to start. By concentrating on academic articles and books and government agencies you will be able to compile information that is relevant to the study you are undertaking. Do not hesitate to ask your instructor about the quality of information you are getting and sources of new information. Much of the information that you find can be compiled as charts and tables (see Chapter 4 of this Manual), thus placing paragraphs that explain the data in appropriate places before and after the charts and tables.

Step 7. Data Analysis.   Your data analysis will be as sophisticated as your knowledge of statistics. At most, you will be able to compile charts that simply display in visible form comparisons of the countries you are studying. See, for example, the charts in Chapter 10 of this manual.

You will find it most helpful to find several recent academic studies similar to the one you are conducting, examine the data analysis methods they employ, and adapt the method you find most appropriate.

Step 8. Compose the Narrative (Thesis).   The narrative of your paper will be composed of three elements: (1) findings, (2) interpretation of findings, and (3) areas for further research. In the findings section of your narrative, you will explain as clearly as possible, with as little interpretation as possible, exactly what the data tells you and what it does not tell you with respect to the research question you are trying to answer. In this section, state clearly what the data *says*, not what it *means*.

The interpretation section of the paper is the most important and the trickiest part of your study. Your paper will be only as valuable as the validity of the conclusions you draw. Be modest. Do not draw conclusions that are not warranted by the data. Try to be as precise as you can in stating the conclusions you have drawn from the information you have found.

In your final section, areas for further research, you may be more expansive than in your interpretation section. Here you can speculate on what you might find if you had more or better data. Here you can suggest new research questions and areas of study that may be helpful in understanding your selected subject matter in the future.

CHAPTER 14

Amicus Curiae Briefs

14.1 Learn the Rules for Writing Briefs for the U.S. Supreme Court

When people are parties to disputes before the U.S. Supreme Court, the attorneys representing each side prepare written documents called *briefs on the merit* that explain the nature of the dispute and present an argument for the side the attorney represents. The justices read the briefs, hear oral arguments, hold conferences to discuss the case, and then write opinions to announce both the Court's decision and the views of justices who disagree in whole or in part with that decision. Cases that come before the Supreme Court are usually important to many people who are not actually parties to the specific case being presented because the Court's decisions contain principles and guidelines that all lower courts must follow in deciding similar cases. *Roe v. Wade*, for example, did not become famous because it allowed one person to have an abortion free from the constraints of the laws of Texas, but because it set forth the principle that state law may not restrict abortions in the first three months of pregnancy to protect the fetus.

Because Supreme Court cases are important to people other than those directly involved in the case, sometimes groups and individuals outside the proceedings of a specific case want their views on cases to be heard by the Court before it makes a decision. It is not proper, however, to go to the justices directly and try to influence them to decide a case in a particular way. Influencing government officials directly through visits, phone calls, or letters is called *lobbying*. When people want to influence the way Congress handles a law, they lobby their representatives by writing letters or talking to them personally. The lobbying of Supreme Court justices, however, is considered improper because the Court is supposed to make decisions based on the content of the Constitution and not on the political preferences of one or more groups in society.

There is a way, however, for outsiders to submit their views to the Supreme Court. The Court invites interested parties, most often organizations, to submit briefs of *amicus curiae* (*amicus curiae* means "friend of the court"). A party that submits an amicus curiae brief becomes a friend of the Court by giving it information that it may find helpful in making a decision. As the Court explains, "an amicus curiae brief which brings relevant matter to the attention of the Court that has not already been brought to its attention by the parties is of considerable help to the Court. An amicus brief which does not serve this purpose simply burdens the staff and facilities of the Court and its filing is not favored" (*Rules of the Supreme Court* 1990, 45).

In the summer of 1971, the Supreme Court began its review of *Roe v. Wade*. Roe, who was arrested for violating a Texas law forbidding abortions except to save the mother's life, argued that the Texas law was a governmental violation of the right to privacy guaranteed to her by the Constitution. Many national organizations filed amicus curiae briefs in this case. Acting as attorneys on behalf of the National Legal Program on Health Problems of the Poor, the National Welfare Rights Organization, and the American Public Health Association, Alan F. Charles and Susan Grossman Alexander filed a brief of amici curiae (*amici* is the plural of *amicus*) in support of the right to an abortion. The Summary of Argument that Charles and Alexander included in that brief appears below as an example to assist you in writing your own amicus curiae brief:

Brief of Amici Curiae

Summary of Argument.   A woman who seeks an abortion is asserting certain fundamental rights, which are protected by the Constitution. Among these are rights to marital and family privacy, to individual and sexual privacy; in sum, the right to choose whether to bear children or not. These rights are abridged by the state's restriction of abortions to saving the mother's life. To justify such an abridgment, the state must demonstrate a compelling interest; no such compelling interest exists to save the Texas abortion law.

The state's interest in protecting the woman's health no longer supports restrictions on abortion. Medical science now performs abortions more safely than it brings a woman through pregnancy and childbirth. Any state interest in discouraging non-marital sexual relationships must be served by laws penalizing these relationships, and not by an indirect, overly broad prohibition on abortion. There is no evidence, in any case, that abortion laws deter such relationships. The state's purported interest in expanding the population lacks any viability today; government policy in every other area is now squarely against it. Any purported interest in permitting all embryos to develop and be born is not supported anywhere in the Constitution or any other body of law.

Because of its restriction, the Texas statute denies to poor and non-white women equal access to legal abortions. It is an undeniable fact that abortion in Texas and in virtually every other state in the United States is far more readily available to the white, paying patient than to the poor and non-white. Studies by physicians, sociologists, public health experts, and lawyers all reach this same conclusion. The reasons for it are not purely economic, i.e., that because abortion is an expensive commodity to obtain on the medical marketplace, it is therefore to be expected that the rich will have greater access to it. It is also because in the facilities, which provide health care to the poor, abortion is simply not made available to the poor and non-white on the same conditions as it is to paying patients. As a result, the poor resort to criminal abortion, with its high toll of infection and death, in vastly disproportionate numbers.

Largely to blame are restrictive abortion laws, such as the Texas statute, in which the legislature has made lay judgments about what conditions must exist before abortions can be legally performed, and has delegated the authority to make such decisions to physicians and committees of physicians with the threat of felony punishment if they err on the side of granting an abortion. Unlike more privileged women, poor and non-white women are unable to shop for physicians and hospitals sympathetic to their applications, cannot afford the necessary consultations to establish that their conditions qualify them for treatment, and must largely depend upon public hospitals and physicians with whom they have no personal relationship, and who operate under the government's eye, for the relief they seek. The resulting discrimination is easily demonstrated.

Restricting abortion only to treatment necessary to save the mother's life irrationally excludes those classes of women for whom abortion is necessary for the protection of health, or because they will bear a deformed fetus, or who are pregnant due to sexual assault, or who are financially, socially or emotionally incapable of raising a child or whose families would be seriously disrupted by the birth of another child, and these exclusions bear most heavily on the poor and non-white.

In the absence of any compelling state interest, the harsh discriminatory effect on the poor and the non-white resulting from the operation of the Texas abortion law denies to poor and non-white women the equal protection of the laws in violation of the Equal Protection Clause of the Fourteenth Amendment. (Charles 1971, 5–7)

Scope and Purpose

Your task in this chapter is to write an amicus curiae brief for a case that is being considered by the U.S. Supreme Court. You will write your own brief, making your own argument about how the case should be decided. Of course, you do not have to be entirely original. You will examine the arguments used in others' briefs, add new arguments of your own, and write the entire brief in your own carefully chosen words. In completing this assignment, you will also be meeting five more personal learning objectives:

1. You will become familiar with the source, form, and content of legal documents.
2. You will become acquainted with the procedures of brief preparation.
3. You will become familiar with the details of a selected case currently before the Court. As you follow the news reports on this case, you will eventually learn the Court's decision.
4. You will come to understand a Supreme Court case in sufficient depth to be able to integrate the arguments of actual amicus curiae briefs into your own argument.
5. You will learn how to write a clear, logical, effective, and persuasive argument.

Remember that your goal is to *persuade* the Supreme Court to make a certain decision. Before you begin, reread Part 1 of this manual, especially the sections on how to write clearly and persuasively.

General Considerations and Format

Briefs provide the Supreme Court with the facts in a particular case and make arguments about how the case should be decided. The *Rules* of the Court state that "a brief must be compact, logically arranged with proper headings, concise, and free from burdensome, irrelevant, immaterial, and scandalous matter. A brief not complying with this paragraph may be disregarded and stricken by the Court" (1990, 28). The Court also requires those who submit an amicus curiae brief to provide a statement of permission, which may be (1) the evidence that either permission to submit the amicus curiae brief has been granted by both parties to the dispute or the permission of both parties has not been granted and (2) the reason for the denial and the reason that the Court should consider the amicus brief in spite of the absence of permission of the parties.

Of course, as a student writing an amicus brief for a class in political science, you will not actually submit your brief to the Supreme Court, so you need not write a statement of permission. Information on such statements is provided here so that you will understand their purpose when you encounter them in your research.

Ask your instructor about the page limit for your assignment. The Supreme Court's limit for the actual text of amicus curiae briefs (exclusive of the questions-presented page, subject index, table of authorities, and appendix) is thirty pages, single-spaced. Your brief, however, will be double-spaced for the convenience of your instructor and as few as fifteen pages, depending on your instructor's requirements. Because a central purpose of this assignment is for you to understand the arguments to be made in the case, your brief will be shorter than actual amicus briefs submitted to the Court, which require much more detail than you will need to know. As you read actual amicus briefs, use your own judgment to select the material that you believe is most important for the Court to understand, and include this information, in your own words, in your brief.

The proper presentation of briefs is essential. Briefs to the Supreme Court are normally professionally printed, and the *Rules* of the Court include directions for this process. The Court does, however, also accept typed briefs, and your amicus curiae brief will conform to the Court's instructions for typed briefs in most respects, with modifications to allow your instructor sufficient space to write comments. You must therefore prepare your amicus curiae brief according to the following specifications:

- Black type on white paper, 81/2 by 11 inches, double-spaced, printed on one side only
- Text and footnotes in 12-point type
- A typeface as close as possible to that used in actual briefs
- Margins of 11/2 inches on the left and 1 inch on all other sides
- A binding that meets your instructor's requirements

You will submit one copy of your brief to your instructor. It is always wise, when submitting any paper, to retain a copy for yourself in case the original is lost. (The Supreme Court requires that sixty copies of a brief be submitted for a case coming to it directly under its original jurisdiction, and forty copies for a case coming to it under appellate jurisdiction from lower courts.)

14.2   Find Resources for Writing an Amicus Brief

You will find resources for amicus curiae briefs on your college library's web page. Look for two periodicals in particular:

■ *Preview of United States Supreme Court Cases*, a publication of the American Bar Association's Public Education Division
■ *The United States Law Week*, published by The Bureau of National Affairs, Inc. If they are not available in your college library, you may request copies through interlibrary loan, or ask your instructor to request that the department or library order them.

To find cases on the Internet that are currently before the Supreme Court, go to Cornell University's Legal Information Institute (LLI) (http://supct.law.cornell.edu/supct/). On this page, you will find a link entitled "Cases Argued This Term." Peruse the links for current cases, selecting the one that most interests you.

14.3   Follow Five Steps for Writing an Amicus Curiae Brief

1. Select a Case and a Side
2. Obtain Copies of the Amicus Briefs
3. Write an Argument Outline
4. Write the Argument
5. Write the Summary of Argument

1. Select a Case and a Side.   Using the most recent issues of *Preview of United States Supreme Court Cases, The United States Law Week*, or Cornell Law site, select a case and decide which side of the argument you support. The case you choose must fulfill the following two requirements:

1. It must be of personal interest to you.
2. It must be a case that has not yet been decided by the Court.

2. Obtain Copies of the Amicus Briefs.   Your next step is to obtain copies of the briefs on the merits of the appellant and the respondent as well as any available amicus briefs on the side of the case that you support and one amicus brief on the opposing side. There are three ways to obtain amicus briefs. You may obtain them by going in person to the Office of the Clerk of the Supreme Court of the United States at the following address, where you will be allowed to photocopy the briefs (the clerk will not send copies of the briefs in the mail):

Office of the Clerk
Supreme Court of the United States
1 First Street, NE
Washington, DC 20543
Telephone: (202) 479-3000

The second way to obtain the briefs is to request them from the attorneys of record for the organizations that are filing the briefs. *Preview of United States Supreme Court Cases* lists their names, addresses, and telephone numbers. *The United States Law Week* provides this information for some cases, but not for all. If this information is not given in either of these publications, you may request it by mail or telephone from the Clerk of the Supreme Court at the above address. Be sure to provide the name and the docket number of the case in which you are interested.

When you contact the attorneys of record, tell them the following:

- Your name and address
- The college or university you attend
- The nature of your assignment
- The name and docket number of the case in which you are interested
- Your interest in obtaining a copy of their amicus brief
- Your appreciation of their assistance

The third way to obtain the briefs, when they are available, is to print or download them from the appropriate sources on the Internet.

3. Write an Argument Outline.   Read the arguments in the briefs you have collected, and then construct an outline of an argument that makes the points you believe are most important. Your outline should normally have from two to six main points. Follow the directions for constructing outlines that you find in Part 1 of this Manual very carefully. Submit your outline to your instructor for advice before continuing.

4. Write the Argument.   Following the outline you have constructed, write your argument. Your writing needs to be clear and sharply focused. Follow the directions for writing in the first part of this manual. The first sentence of each paragraph should state its main point.

The *Rules* of the Court state that the argument of a brief must exhibit "clearly the points of fact and of law being presented and [cite] the authorities and statutes relied upon"; it should also be "as short as possible" (1990, 27). In addition to conforming to page limitations set by your instructor, the length of your argument should be guided by two considerations. First, content must be of adequate length to help the Court make a good decision. All the arguments necessary to making a decision must be present. Write this paper as if you were an officer of the Court. Under no circumstances should you make a false or misleading statement. Be persuasive, but be truthful. You do not need to make the opponents' argument for them, but the facts that you present must be accurate to the best of your knowledge.

The second guideline for determining the length of your argument is to omit extraneous material. Include only the information that will be of help to the Court in making the decision at hand.

The *Rules* of the Court require that an amicus brief include a "conclusion, specifying with particularity the relief which the party seeks" (1990, 27). Read the conclusions of the briefs you collect, and then write your own, retaining the same format but combining the arguments for the groups you are representing, and limiting your conclusion to two pages.

5. Write the Summary of Argument.   After you have written the argument, write the summary, which should be a clearly written series of paragraphs that include all the main points. It should be brief, not more than three double-spaced typed pages. The Summary of Argument written for *Roe* v. *Wade* that is included at the beginning of this chapter provides an example.

According to the *Rules* of the Court, briefs should contain a "summary of the argument, suitably paragraphed, which should be a succinct, but accurate and clear, condensation of the argument actually made in the body of the brief. A mere repetition of the headings under which the argument is arranged is not sufficient" (1990, 27).

The summary of your argument may be easily assembled by taking the topic sentences from each paragraph and forming them into new paragraphs. The topic sentences contain more information than your subject headings. As complete sentences arranged in logical order, they provide an excellent synopsis of the contents of your brief. Your argument summary should not exceed two double-spaced pages.

List of Political Science Periodicals

Administration and Society

Administrative Science Quarterly

African Affairs

Africa Quarterly

Alternatives: A Journal for World Policy

American Behavioral Scientist

American Journal of International Law

American Journal of Political Science

American Political Science Review

American Politics Quarterly

Annals of the American Academy of
  Political and Social Science

Armed Forces and Society

Asian Affairs

Asian Quarterly

Asian Survey

Atlantic Community Quarterly

Australian Journal of Politics and History

Australian Journal of Public
  Administration

Behavioral Science

Behavior Science Research

Black Politician

British Journal of International Studies

British Journal of Law and Society

British Journal of Political Science

Bureaucrat

Campaign and Elections

Canadian Journal of Behavioral Science

Canadian Journal of Political Science

Canadian Public Administration

Canadian Public Policy

China Quarterly

Communist Affairs

Comparative Political Studies

Comparative Politics

Comparative Strategy

Comparative Studies in Society
  and History

Conflict

Conflict Bulletin

Conflict Management and Peace Science

Conflict Studies

Congress and the Presidency

Contemporary China

Cooperation and Conflict

Daedalus

Democracy

Development and Change

Diplomatic History

Dissent

East European Quarterly

Electoral Studies

Environmental Policy and Law

European Journal of Political Research

European Journal of Political Science

European Studies Review

Experimental Study of Politics

Foreign Affairs

Foreign Policy

General Systems

German Foreign Policy

German Political Studies

Global Political Assessment

Governance: An International Journal of Policy and Administration

Government & Opposition

Government Finance

Growth and Change

Harvard Journal on Legislation

History and Theory

History of Political Thought

Human Organization

Human Relations

Human Rights Review

Indian Journal of Political Science

Indian Journal of Public Administration

Indian Political Science Review

International Affairs

International Development Review

International Interactions

International Journal of Political Education

International Journal of Public Administration

International Organization

International Political Science Review (Revue Internationale de Science Politique)

International Relations

International Review of Social History

International Security

International Studies

International Studies Quarterly

Interpretation: Journal of Political Philosophy

Jerusalem Journal of International Relations

Journal of African Studies

Journal of Applied Behavioral Science

Journal of Asian Studies

Journal of Common Market Studies

Journal of Commonwealth and Comparative Politics

Journal of Conflict Resolution

Journal of Constitutional and Parliamentary Studies

Journal of Contemporary History

Journal of Developing Areas

Journal of Development Studies

Journal of European Integration

Journal of Health Politics, Policy, and Law

Journal of International Affairs

Journal of Japanese Studies

Journal of Law & Politics

Journal of Libertarian Studies

Journal of Modern African Studies

Journal of Modern History

Journal of Peace Research

Journal of Peace Science

Journal of Policy Analysis and Management

Journal of Policy Modeling

Journal of Political and Military Sociology

Journal of Political Economy

Journal of Political Science

Journal of Politics

Journal of Public Policy

Journal of Social History

Journal of Social Issues

Journal of Social, Political, and Economic Studies

Journal of Strategic Studies

Journal of the History of Ideas

Journal of Theoretical Politics

Journal of Urban Analysis

Law and Contemporary Problems

Law and Policy Quarterly

Law & Society Review

Legislative Studies Quarterly

Mathematical Social Sciences

Micropolitics

Middle Eastern Studies

Middle East Journal

Millennium

Modern China

Multivariate Behavioral Research

New Political Science

Orbis: A Journal of World Affairs

Pacific Affairs

Parliamentarian

Parliamentary Affairs

Parliaments, Estates, and Representation

Peace and Change

Peace Research

Perspectives on Political Science

Philosophy & Public Affairs

Philosophy of the Social Sciences

Planning and Administration

Policy Analysis

Policy and Politics

Policy Review

Policy Sciences

Policy Studies Journal

Policy Studies Review

Political Anthropology

Political Behavior

Political Communication and Persuasion

Political Geography Quarterly

Political Psychology

Political Quarterly

Political Science

Political Science Quarterly

Political Science Review

Political Science Reviewer

Political Studies

Political Theory

Politics

Politics & Society

Polity

Presidential Studies Quarterly

Public Administration (Australia)

Public Administration (United States)

Public Administration Review

Public Choice

Public Finance

Public Finance Quarterly

Public Interest

Public Law

Public Opinion Quarterly

Public Policy

Publius: The Journal of Federalism

Quarterly Journal of Administration

Res Publica

Review of International Studies (formerly
   British Journal of International Studies)

Review of Law and Social Change

Review of Politics

Revolutionary World

Round Table

Russian Review

Scandinavian Political Studies

Science and Public Affairs

Science and Public Policy

Science and Society

Simulation and Games

Slavic Review

Slavonic and East European Review

Social Forces

Social Indicators Research

Socialism and Democracy

Social Policy

Social Praxis

Social Research

Social Science Journal

Social Science Quarterly

Social Science Research

Social Theory and Practice

Sociological Analysis and Theory

Sociological Methods and Research

Sociology and Social Research

Southeastern Political Science Review

Soviet Review

Soviet Studies

Soviet Union

Strategic Review

Studies in Comparative Communism

Studies in Comparative International
Development

Survey

Talking Politics

Technological Forecasting and Social Change

Terrorism

Theory and Decision

Theory and Society

Third World

Urban Affairs Quarterly

Urban Studies

War & Society

Washington Quarterly: A Review of
Strategic and International Studies

Western Political Quarterly

West European Politics

Wilson Quarterly

Women & Politics: A Quarterly Journal of
Research and Policy Studies

World Development

World Policy Journal

World Politics

Youth and Society

Table of Forms of Proper Address Formats

This table was adapted from Appendix 6 of the *Department of Defense Manual for Written Material* (March 2, 2004, Director of Administration and Management, Office of the Secretary of Defense). It provides proper address formats for a wide variety of elected and nonelected public officials at local, state, national, and international levels of government.

Addressee	Address on Letter and Envelope	Salutation and Close
The President	The President The White House 1600 Pennsylvania Avenue, NW Washington, DC 20500	Dear Mr./Madam President: Respectfully yours,
Spouse of the President	Mr./Mrs. (full name) The White House 1600 Pennsylvania Avenue, NW Washington, DC 20500	Dear Mr./Mrs. (surname): Sincerely,
Director, Office of Management and Budget	The Honorable (full name) Director, Office of Management and Budget Washington, DC 20503	Dear Mr./Ms. (surname): Sincerely,
The Vice President	The Vice President 276 Eisenhower Executive Office Building Washington, DC 20501	Dear Mr./Madam Vice President: Sincerely,
The Chief Justice	The Chief Justice The Supreme Court Washington, DC 20543	Dear Chief Justice: Sincerely,
Associate Justice	The Honorable (full name) The Supreme Court Washington, DC 20543	Dear Justice (Surname): Sincerely,

Addressee	Address on Letter and Envelope	Salutation and Close
Judge of a federal, state, or local court	The Honorable (full name) Judge of the (name of court) (address)	Dear Judge (surname): Sincerely,
Clerk of a court	Mr. (full name) Clerk of the (name of court)(address)	Dear Mr./Ms. (surname): Sincerely,
Senator (Washington office)	The Honorable (full name) United States Senate Washington, DC 20510-(+4 Code)	Dear Senator (surname): Sincerely,
Speaker of the House of Representatives	The Honorable (full name) Speaker of the House of Representatives U.S. House of Representatives Washington, DC 20515-(+4 Code)	Dear Mr./Madam Speaker: Sincerely,
Representative (Washington office)	The Honorable (full name) U.S. House of Representatives Washington, DC 20515-(+4 Code)	Dear Representative (surname): Sincerely,
Resident Commissioner	The Honorable (full name) Resident Commissioner from Puerto Rico U.S. House of Representatives Washington, DC 20515-(+4 Code)	Dear Mr./Ms. (surname): Sincerely,
Delegate	The Honorable (full name) Delegate from (location) U.S. House of Representatives Washington, DC 20515-(+4 Code)	Dear Mr./Ms. (surname): Sincerely,
Members of the Cabinet addressed as Secretary	The Honorable (full name) Secretary of (name of Department) Washington, DC (ZIP+4 Code)	Dear Mr./Madam Secretary: Sincerely,
Attorney General	The Honorable (full name) Attorney General Washington, DC 20530	Dear Mr. Attorney General: Sincerely,

Addressee	Address on Letter and Envelope	Salutation and Close
Deputy Secretary of a department	The Honorable (full name) Deputy Secretary of (name of Department) Washington, DC (ZIP+4 Code)	Dear Mr./Ms. (surname): Sincerely,
Head of a federal agency, authority, or board	The Honorable (full name) (title) (agency) Washington, DC (ZIP+4 Code)	Dear Mr./Ms. (surname): Sincerely,
President of a commission or board	The Honorable (full name) President, (name of commission) Washington, DC (ZIP+4 Code)	Dear Mr./Ms. (surname): Sincerely,
Chairman of a commission or board	The Honorable (full name) Chairman, (name of commission) Washington, DC (ZIP+4 Code)	Dear Mr./Madam Chairman: Sincerely,
Postmaster General	The Honorable (full name) Postmaster General 475 L'Enfant Plaza West, SW Washington, DC 20260	Dear Mr./Madam Postmaster General: Sincerely,
American Ambassador	The Honorable (full name) American Ambassador (city) (city), (country)	Dear Mr./Madam Ambassador: Sincerely,
Foreign ambassador in the United States	His/Her Excellency (full name) Ambassador of (country)Washington, DC (ZIP+4 Code)	Dear Mr./Madam Ambassador: Sincerely,
Secretary General of the United Nations	The Honorable (full name) Secretary General of the United Nations New York, NY 10017	Dear Mr./Madam Secretary General: Sincerely,
United States Representative to the United Nations	The Honorable (full name) United States Representative to the United Nations New York, NY 10017	Dear Mr./Ms. (surname): Sincerely,

Addressee	Address on Letter and Envelope	Salutation and Close
State Governor	The Honorable (full name) Governor of (state) (city) (state) (ZIP Code)	Dear Governor (surname): Sincerely,
State Lieutenant Governor	The Honorable (full name) Lieutenant Governor of (state) (city), (state) (ZIP Code)	Dear Mr./Ms. (surname): Sincerely,
State Secretary of State	The Honorable (full name) Secretary of State of (state) (city), (state) (ZIP Code)	Dear Mr./Madam (surname): Sincerely,
Chief Justice of a State Supreme Court	The Honorable (full name) Chief Justice Supreme Court of the State of (state) (city), (state) (ZIP Code)	Dear Mr./Madam Chief Justice: Sincerely,
State Attorney General	The Honorable (full name) Attorney General State of (state) (city), (state) (ZIP Code)	Dear Mr./Madam Attorney General: Sincerely,
State Treasurer, Comptroller, or Auditor	The Honorable (full name) State Treasurer (Comptroller) (Auditor) State of (state) (city), (state) (ZIP Code)	Dear Mr./Ms. (surname): Sincerely,
President, State Senate	The Honorable (full name) President of the Senate of the State of (state) (city), (state) (ZIP Code)	Dear Mr./Ms. (surname): Sincerely,
State Senator	The Honorable (full name)\ (state) Senate (city), (state) (ZIP Code)	Dear Mr./Ms. (surname): Sincerely,
Speaker, State House of Representatives, Assembly or House of Delegates	The Honorable (full name) Speaker of the House of Representatives (Assembly) (House of Delegates) of the State of (state) (city), (state) (ZIP Code)	Dear Mr./Ms. (surname): Sincerely,

Addressee	Address on Letter and Envelope	Salutation and Close
State Representative, Assemblyman, or Delegate	The Honorable (full name) (state) House of Representatives (Assembly) (House of Delegates) (city), (state) (ZIP Code)	Dear Mr./Ms. (surname): Sincerely,
Mayor	The Honorable (full name) Mayor of (city)(city), (state) (ZIP Code)	Dear Mayor (surname) Sincerely,
President of a Board of Commissioners	The Honorable (full name) President, Board of Commissioners of (city) (city), (state) (ZIP Code)	Dear Mr./Ms. (surname): Sincerely,

Bibliography

Agassiz, Louis. 1958. *A Scientist of Two Worlds: Louis Agassiz.* Ed. Catherine Owens Pearce. Philadelphia: Lippincott.

Almond, Gabriel. 1990. *A Discipline Divided, Schools and Sects in Political Science.* Newbury Park, Calif.: Sage Publications.

Bary, William Theodore de, Wing-tsit Chan, and Burton Wilson, comps. 1966. *Sources of Chinese Tradition.* New York: Columbia University Press.

Brundage, D., R. Keane, and R. Mackneson. 1993. "Application of Learning Theory to the Instruction of Adults." In *The Craft of Teaching Adults.* Ed. Thelma Barer-Stein and James A. Draper, 131–44. Toronto: Culture Concepts.

Buchanan, James. 1972. "Toward Analysis of Closed Behavioral Systems." In *Theory of Public Choice.* Ed. James M. Buchanan and Robert D. Tollison. Ann Arbor: University of Michigan Press.

Buchanan, James. 1972. "The Inconsistencies of the National Health Service." In *Theory of Public Choice.* Ed. James M. Buchanan and Robert D. Tollison. Ann Arbor: University of Michigan Press.

Charles, Alan F. 1971. *Motion for Leave to File Brief Amici Curiae in Support of Appellants and Briefs Amici Curiae. Roe v. Wade.* U.S. 70–18, 5–7.

Chicago Manual of Style. 1993. 14th ed. Chicago, IL: University of Chicago Press.

Chicago Manual of Style. 2003. 15th ed. Chicago, IL: University of Chicago Press.

Crick, Bernard. 1960. *The American Science of Politics Its Origins and Conditions.* Berkeley: University of California Press.

Esposito, John L., ed. 1997. *Political Islam: Revolution, Radicalism, or Reform?* Boulder, CO: Lynne Rienner Publishers.

Foucault, Michel. 1995. *Discipline and Punish: The Birth of the Prison.* New York: Vintage Books.

Hartwell, Patrick. 1985. "Grammar, Grammars, and the Teaching of Grammar." *College English* 47:105–27.

Hochenauer, Kurt. 2010. "False Comparison." *Okie Funk: Notes From the Outback.* Blog. Okiefunk.com

Huffington Post. 2008. *The Huffington Post Complete Guide to Blogging.* New York: Simon & Schuster.

Kahn, Kim Fridkin. 1994. "Does Gender Make a Difference? An Experimental Examination of Sex Stereotypes and Press Patterns in Statewide Campaigns." *American Journal of Political Science* 38:162–95.

Kennedy, John F. 1963. "John F. Kennedy's Inaugural Address." In *Documents of American History Since 1898.* Vol. 2 of *Documents of American History.* 7th ed. Ed. Henry Steele Commager, 688–89. New York: Appleton-Century-Crofts.

Laitin, David D. 2002. "Comparative Politics: The State of the Subdiscipline." In *Political Science: The State of the Discipline.* Eds. Ira Katznelson and Helen V. Milner. New York: W.W. Nelson.

Lieber, Francis. 1881. "An Inaugural Address Delivered on the 17th of February, 1858, on Assuming the Chair of History and Political Science, in Columbia College, New York." In *Miscellaneous Writings.* Vol. 1. Philadelphia: J.B. Lippincott.

Lowi, Theodore J. 1993. *The State in Political Science: How We Become What We Study.* Ann Arbor: University of Michigan Press.

Lunsford, Andrea, and Robert Connors. 1992. *The St. Martin's Handbook.* 2nd ed. Annotated instructor's ed. New York: St. Martin's.

Machiavelli, Niccolo. 1979. *The Prince.* In *The Portable Machiavelli.* Trans. Peter Bondanella and Mark Musa. New York: Viking Press.

Madison, James, Alexander Hamilton, and John Jay. 1961. *The Federalist Papers.* New York: New American Library/Mentor.

Park, Andrus. 1994 "Ethnicity and Independence: The Case of Estonia in Comparative Perspective." *Europe-Asia Studies* 46:69–87.

Roosevelt, Franklin D. 1963. "F. D. Roosevelt's First Inaugural Address." In *Documents of American History Since 1898.* Vol. 2. 7th ed. Ed. Henry Steele Commager, 239–42. New York: Appleton-Century-Crofts.

Rules of the Supreme Court of the United States. 1990. Washington, DC: Government Printing Office.

Scott, Gregory M. 1998. Review of *Political Islam: Revolution, Radicalism, or Reform?* Ed. John L. Esposito. *Southeastern Political Review* 26(2): 512–14.

Style Manual for Political Science. 2006. Rev. ed. Washington, D.C.: American Political Science Association.

Washington, George. 1991. *Washington's Farewell Address to the People of the United States.* 102d Cong., 1st sess. S. Doc. 3.

Glossary of Political Science Terms

Affirmative action   The correcting of discrimination, usually racial in motivation, through government policy

Amendment   A formal action taken by the legislature to change an existing law or bill

Amicus curiae brief   A "friend of the court" brief, filed by a third party to a lawsuit who is presenting additional information to the court in the hopes of influencing the court's decision

Anarchism   The belief that all political authority is inherently oppressive and that government should be reduced to a minimum

Anarchy   Political chaos; as a political movement, the belief that voluntary cooperation among members of a society is better than any form of organized government, because government generally favors one group over others

Antifederalist   One who opposed ratification of the United States Constitution in 1787

Antinomianism   A belief that faith without adherence to law is sufficient for religious practice

Appeal   The process of asking a higher court to consider a verdict rendered by a lower court

Apportionment   The system under which seats in the legislative houses are apportioned among the states

Appropriation   The act of designating funds in the legislature for particular agencies and programs

APSA   American Political Science Association

Aristocracy   A system of government in which power is held by a small ruling class whose status is determined by such factors as wealth, social position, and military power

Authoritarianism   Rule without popular consent, requiring obedience to law but not necessarily active support for a regime

Authority   The power to make, interpret, and enforce laws

Autocratic   Having unrestricted power

Autonomous   Self-governing; independent

Balance of Power   A relationship between or among nations in which combinations of strengths and advantages create a situation in which no one nation achieves hegemony

Bandwagon effect   The practice of government officials' attaching themselves to a piece of legislation or a political movement because of its popularity

Bicameral legislature   A legislature that is divided into two branches or houses

Blog   A web-log, or discussion carried on by successive entries and numerous parties on an internet site

Bipolar   An international system dominated by two countries, such as the U.S. and the U.S.S.R. during the Cold War

Bourgeoisie   For Karl Marx, the capitalist middle class

Brief   A compilation of facts, arguments, and points of law concerning a specific law case, prepared by an attorney and submitted to the court

Bureaucracy   Any large, complex administrative system, but used most often to refer to government in general

Calendar   The agenda listing the business to be taken up by a legislative body

Capitalism   An economic system in which the means of production and distribution are privately owned and operated for profit

Case study   A detailed examination of a representative individual or group

Caucus   A closed meeting of party officials for the purpose of selecting candidates for government office

Censure   A method by which a legislative body may discipline one of its members

Census   The counting, every ten years, of the total population of the United States, for such purposes as the apportionment of legislators and the determination of direct taxes

Centralization   The concept of focusing power in a national government instead of in state or local governments

Checks and balances   A method of government power distribution in which each major branch of the government has some control over the actions of the other major branches

Circuit court   A superior court that hears civil and criminal cases, and whose judges serve in courts in several jurisdictions or counties, thus going on the "circuit"

Civil rights   The rights of a citizen that guarantee protection against discriminatory behavior by the government or private owners of public facilities

Civil servants   Government employees who are not in the military

Claims court   A court that hears various kinds of claims brought by citizens against the government

Class stratification   The differentiation of classes within a society for political or economic purposes

Closed primary   A primary election in which only party members may vote

Cloture (closure)   A rule allowing a three-fifths vote of the Senate to end a filibuster

Coattail effect   The tendency of a candidate or officeholder to draw votes for other candidates of his or her party

Cognitive dissonance   A perceived discrepancy between what is stated to be reality and what is reality in fact

Collectivism   An economic system in which the land and the means of production and distribution are owned by the people who operate them

Commerce clause   A clause in Article 1, section 8, of the U.S. Constitution, giving Congress the power to regulate trade among the states and with foreign nations

Communism   A collectivist social system in which the means of production are owned by the state and in which the products of society are distributed according to need

Communitarian   One who advocates communal life, in which possessions are shared by commune members

Concurrent powers   Powers shared by state and national governments, including the power to tax and the power to maintain a system of courts

Confederacy   A political system characterized by a weak national government that assumes only those powers granted it by strong state governments

Conservatism   An ideology normally associated with resistance to changes in culture, and less government intervention in the social and economic life of the nation

Conservatives   Citizens who resist major changes in their culture and their society; political conservatives tend to favor less government intervention in the social and economic life of the nation

Constituent   An individual who resides in a government official's electoral district

Constitutionalism   A belief in a system of government limited and controlled by a constitution, or contract, drawn up and agreed to by its citizens

Contract theory   An explanation of the relationship of the government to the governed in terms of contractual obligation by consenting parties

Corporatism   An approach to the study of politics focusing on the activities of economic interests

Court of appeals   One of twelve national courts in the United States set up to hear appeals from district courts

Cybernetics   The study of government that focuses on how information is transmitted and received

Dark horse   A candidate for political office who has little chance of winning

Deductive logic   Reasoning from a general premise to a specific conclusion

Demagogue   A political leader who obtains popularity through emotional appeals to the prejudices and fears of the voters

Democracy   A system of government in which the majority governs and in which the rights of minorities are protected

Deregulation   The process of reducing government regulatory involvement in private business

Detente   The relaxing of tension between nations

Dialectic   A process of arriving at the truth in which succeeding propositions transform each other

District court   The most basic federal court, where federal cases generally are first heard

Divine right   The belief that a ruler maintains power through a mandate from a Supreme Being

Due process   The right accorded to American citizens to expect fair and equitable treatment in the processes and procedures of law

Eclectic   Combining a variety of approaches or methods

Electoral college   Electors who meet in their respective state capitals to elect the president and vice president of the United States

Elite theory   The concept that, in any political system, power is always controlled by a small group of people

Empiricism   The idea that all knowledge results from sense experience; a scientific method that relies on direct observation

Epistemology   The study of what knowledge is

Ethnocentricity   A tendency to believe that one's own race is superior to other races; a focus of attention upon one race, to the exclusion of others

Faction   A group of people sharing certain beliefs who seek to act together to affect policy

Fascism   A totalitarian political system in which power is concentrated in the hands of a dictator who keeps rigid control of society and promotes a belligerent nationalism

Favorite son   A presidential candidate, usually with no chance of winning the party nomination, whose name is placed in nomination at the national convention by the person's home state, usually either to honor that individual or to allow the state's delegation to delay committing their votes to a viable candidate

Federal   A type of government in which power is shared by state and national governments

Filibuster   The Senate process of interrupting meaningful debate on a bill with prolonged, irrelevant speeches aimed at "talking the bill to death"

Flow model   A diagram illustrating the relationships among elements of a system

Franking privilege   The ability of a member of Congress to substitute his or her facsimile signature for a postage stamp and thereby send mail free of charge

Gag rule   A rule limiting the amount of time that can be spent debating a bill or resolution in the legislature

Gaia hypothesis   James Lovelock's conservationist concept of the earth as a living entity needing the same sort of nurture that all organisms require

Game theory   A method of understanding and predicting sociopolitical attitudes and events through devising mathematical models of social behavior

Gerrymandering   Redesigning the boundaries of a legislative district so that the political party controlling the state legislature can maintain control

Grand jury   A group of twelve to twenty-three citizens selected to hear evidence against persons accused of a serious crime in order to determine whether or not a formal charge should be issued

Grants-in-aid   Funding given to state and local governments for them to achieve goals set by the national government

Green   In politics, a name for those policies, politicians, and activists who advocate environmental responsibility in policy decisions

Habeas corpus   A court order requiring that an individual in custody be presented in court with the cause of his or her detention

Hard left   In Gabriel Almond's methodological approach to the study of politics, the mode that stresses the scientific analysis of quantitative data in the interests of promoting social, economic, and political equality

Hard right   The method of studying politics, in Gabriel Almond's research, that stresses the scientific analysis of quantitative data and rational thinking and focuses on the study of power

Hegemony   A situation in international relations in which one nation dominates the others

Humanism   The concept that humanity, and not a deity, is and should be the central focus of concern in philosophy, politics, the arts, etc.

Ideology   The combined beliefs and doctrines that reveal an individual's or a culture's value system

Impeachment   The process by which the lower house of a legislature may accuse a high official, such as the president or a Supreme Court justice, of a crime, after which the official is tried by the upper house

Implied powers   Powers held by the federal government that are not specified in the U.S. Constitution but are implied by other, enumerated powers

Incumbent   A political official currently in office

Independent   A voter not registered as a member of a political party

Indictment   A formal accusation, brought by a grand jury, charging a person with a crime

Individualism   The belief in the importance of the needs and rights of the individual over those of the group

Inductive logic   Reasoning from a series of specific observations to a general principle

Inefficient game   In game theory, a game in which no player completely achieves a desired end

Inherent powers   Powers not specified in the U.S. Constitution that are claimed by the president, especially in foreign relations

Initiative   A process by which individuals or interested groups may draw up proposed legislation and bring it to the attention of the legislature through a petition signed by a certain percentage of registered voters

Interest group   An organization of like-minded individuals seeking to influence the making of government policy, often by sponsoring a political action committee (PAC)

Intrasocietal   The environment existing inside the structure of a given society

Iron curtain   Those countries of Eastern Europe dominated by the Soviet Union

Iron law of oligarchy   The principle stating that all associations eventually become dominated by a minority of their members

Iron triangle   The interrelationship of government agencies, congressional committees, and political action groups as they influence policy

Irrationalist   One who believes that human behavior is determined by factors other than reason

Item veto   The power of governors in most states to veto selected items from a bill and to approve others

Knesset   The legislative body of the Israeli government

Laissez-faire   A "hands-off" policy rejecting government involvement in the economic system of a state

Left wing   An outlook favoring liberal political and economic programs aimed at benefiting the masses

Legitimacy   The quality of being accepted as authentic; in politics, the people's acceptance of a form of government

Libel   A written statement aimed at discrediting an individual's reputation. See also Slander

Liberals   Citizens who favor changes in the system of government to benefit the common people

Libertarians   Advocates of freedom from government action

Linkage   In international relations, when two or more issues are always discussed with reference to the others

Literature review   In a research project, the task of canvassing publications, usually professional journals, in order to find information about a specific topic

Lobbyists   People who seek to influence legislation for the benefit of themselves or their clients—usually interest groups—by applying pressure of various kinds to members of Congress

Logrolling   A process by which two or more legislators agree to support each other's bills, which usually concern public works projects

Majority rule   The concept, common in a democracy, that the majority has the right to govern

Millenarian   Member of any of many religious movements that challenged the church after the year CE 1000

Millennium   A period of 1,000 years

Moderate   Within reasonable limits; in politics, one who is opposed to extremely liberal or conservative views

Monarchy   A political system in which power is held by a hereditary aristocracy, headed by a king or queen

Multipolar   An international system in which three or more nations have substantial strategic advantages

Myth   A story or narrative intended to explain a natural or social phenomenon beyond normal human understanding

Naturalization   The process by which an alien becomes an American citizen

Natural law   The concept, popularized by eighteenth-century philosophers, that human conduct is governed by immutable laws that are similar to the laws of the physical universe and can, like physical laws, be discovered

Nazism   The political movement led in Germany by Adolf Hitler, combining nationalism with anti-Semitism

Negative freedom   Isaiah Berlin's phrase for the freedom from obligation or restraint on one's actions

Neoconservatism   A conservative reaction to liberal and radical movements of the 1960s

Nepotism   The policy of granting political favors, such as government contracts or jobs, to family members

New Left   A liberal political movement begun in the 1960s, largely due to the civil rights movement and the Vietnam War, that brought about widespread reevaluation of political beliefs

Normative theory   Any theory attempting to assign value judgments to its conclusions, as opposed to quantitative theory, which attempts to produce value-free results

Oligarchy   A political system in which power is held by a small group whose membership is determined by wealth or social position

Open primary   A primary election in which voters need not disclose their party affiliation to cast a ballot

Orthodox   "Right belief," holding the basic beliefs of the faith. A model or example

Panopticon   A model prison designed by philosopher Jeremy Bentham and used by philosopher Michel Foucault as a metaphor for freedom in society

Paradigm   A member of the wealthy class or aristocracy

Patrician   The study of the development of human consciousness and how it attempts to assimilate sensory data

Patronage   The power of government officeholders to dole out jobs, contracts, and other favors in return for political support

Phenomenology   In common use, of the common people, as opposed to the aristocracy

Pigeonhole   The action of a congressional committee that, by failing to report a bill out for general consideration, assures its demise

Platform   The set of principles and goals on which a political party or group bases its appeal to the public

Plebeian   Ordering societal relations

Pluralism   The concept that cultural, ethnic, and political diversity plays a major part in the development of government policy

Plurality   The number of votes by which a candidate wins election if that number does not exceed 50 percent of the total votes cast; a plurality need not be a large number of votes, as long as it is a higher number than that claimed by any other candidate

Pocket veto   A method by which the president may kill a bill simply by failing to sign it within ten days following the end of a legislative session

Police power   The power, reserved to legislatures, to establish order and implement government policy

Political action committees (PACs)   Officially registered fund-raising committees that attempt to influence legislation, usually through campaign contributions to members of Congress

Political correctness   A measure of how closely speech, attitude, or policy conforms to certain affirmative action standards. The term is pejorative when used by conservatives warning of liberal attempts at controlling the public's modes of expression and thought processes

Political machine   A political party organization so well established as to wield considerable power

Political party   An organization of officeholders, political candidates, and workers, all of whom share a particular set of beliefs and work together to gain political power through the electoral process

Politics polity   For Aristotle, government by the many in the interests of all

Poll   A survey undertaken to ascertain the opinions of a section of the public

Poll sample   A selection, usually random, of the larger population of individuals polled

Populism   A political philosophy that aims at representing the needs of the rural and poor populations in the United States rather than the interests of the upper classes and big business

Pork barrel legislation   A congressional bill passed to benefit one specific congressional district, with the aim of promoting the reelection of representatives from that district

Positive freedom   Isaiah Berlin's phrase for the freedom to do what one wills

Pragmatism   The notion that ideas and concepts should be judged by their practical consequences instead of their correspondence to abstract or ideal criteria

Precedent   A court decision that sets a standard for handling later, similar cases

Primary election   An election, held prior to the general election, in which voters nominate party candidates for office

Progressivism   Any doctrine calling for changes within a system, to be made in light of recent findings or achievements

Proletariat   The urban, industrial working class

Quantification   Determining or measuring quantity or amount

Quorum   The minimum number of members of a legislative body that must be present to conduct business

Radical   One calling for substantial change in institutions, society, political systems, etc.

Ratification   The process by which state legislatures approve or reject proposed agreements between states and proposed amendments to the U.S. Constitution

Rational actor theory   In public policy analysis, the theory that people and institutions tend to act in ways which they perceive to be in their own best interests

Rationalism   The belief that reasoned observation is the proper foundation for problem solving

Reactionary   One who opposes liberal change, favoring instead a return to policies of the past

Recall   A process by which an elected official can be turned out of office through a popular vote

Recidivism   A tendency for criminal offenders to return to criminal habits

Referendum   Method by which voters in certain states can register their approval or dissatisfaction with a bill proposed in their state legislature

Regime   A system of formal and informal power arrangements through which political power is applied, either in domestic or international affairs

Republic   A government that derives its power from the consent of the people, who control policy by electing government officeholders

Reserved powers   Powers of the U.S. Constitution reserved to the state governments

Right wing   An outlook favoring conservative or reactionary political and economic programs

Sample plan   An essential step in setting up a survey; the task of establishing which elements of the general population are to be asked to participate in the survey

Sampling frame   That specific part of a population from which a sample is drawn for a survey

Separation of powers   A method of stabilizing a government by dividing its power among different branches or levels of government

Short ballot   A ballot listing candidates for only a few offices, as opposed to a long ballot, which lists candidates for a great number of offices

Single-issue group   A lobby group attempting to influence legislation concerning only one cause or issue, such as gun control or funding for education

Single-member district   An electoral district from which voters elect only a single representative

Slander   An oral statement intended to damage an individual's reputation. See also Libel

Social contract   The agreement, either formally stated or implied, among members of a society that allows for the establishment and continuance of the social structure and the government

Socialism   An economic system in which the state owns the means of production

Soft left   In Gabriel Almond's terms, a methodological approach to the study of politics which favors philosophical and descriptive analysis of political in the interests of social, economic, or political equality

Soft right   The analytical mode described by Gabriel Almond that takes a philosophical or descriptive rather than a quantitative approach to the study of power and rational thinking in politics

Sovereignty   The concept that the state is self-governing and free from external control

Soviet Bloc   Those Eastern European countries dominated by Soviet communism from 1945 to 1990

Split ticket   A situation in which a voter casts ballots for candidates from different political parties

Spoils system   The practice of rewarding supporters and friends with government jobs

Stalking horse   A candidate whose primary function is to set up a constituency and a campaign base for another candidate, deemed stronger by the party, who will be announced later

Statute   A law passed by Congress or a state legislature

Straight ticket   The practice of voting for all candidates on a ballot solely on the basis of their party affiliation

Structural-functionalism   A method of studying political systems introduced by Gabriel Almond in which various elements of a political system are analyzed according to the types of tasks they perform

Subjectivism   A theory of knowledge in which truth is individually determined by each person's preferences or perceptions

Theocracy   A political system whose leaders assume that their power to govern comes from a Supreme Being who guides the actions of the government

Third party   A political party different from the two traditional parties and typically formed to protest their ineffectualness

Totalitarianism   A type of authoritarian government in which the state demands active support of its policies

Typology   A classification of phenomena according to differing characteristics

Unicameralism   A legislature with only one house or chamber

Unipolar   An international system in which one nation dominates the others. See hegemony

Unitary   Referring to a political system in which all power resides in the national government, which in turn delegates limited power to local governments

Utopia   An ideal social environment

Validity   In statistics, the characteristic that a measuring instrument, such as a survey, has when it actually measures what it purports to measure

Variables   The elements of an equation, experiment, or formula that are under study and subject to change in accordance with changes in their environment

Veil of Ignorance   A hypothetical state, proposed by philosopher John Rawls, in which people, before beginning their lives, are unaware of what characteristics, advantages, and disadvantages they will have in life

Veto   The process by which the president may send a bill back to Congress instead of signing it into law

Welfare state   A state in which the government is characterized by governmental redistribution of income

Index

Notes

Notes

Notes

Notes

Notes

Notes

Notes

Notes

Notes